THE GREEN DESERT

The Green Desert

A Silent Retreat

Rita Winters

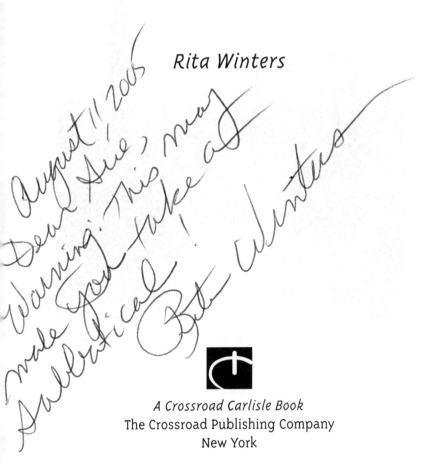

August 11, 2006

Dear Sue, may
Warning: This may
make you take a
Sabbatical!

Rita Winters

A Crossroad Carlisle Book
The Crossroad Publishing Company
New York

The Crossroad Publishing Company
16 Penn Plaza, 481 Eighth Avenue, New York, NY 10001

This book is set in 13/17 Bitstream Venetian 301 Demi.
The display type is Triplex Serif.

Printed in the United States of America

Library of Congress Cataloging-in-Publication Data
Winters, Rita, 1951-
    The green desert : a silent retreat / Rita Winters.
        p. cm.
    "A Crossroad Carlisle book."
    "A retreat reading list": P.
    ISBN 0-8245-2133-1
    1. Spiritual retreats – Catholic Church. 2. Winters, Rita, 1951-
I. Title.
    BX2375.W56 2004
    269'.6 – dc22

                                                        2003021943

1   2   3   4   5   6   7   8   9   10   10   09   08   07   06   05   04

For Fabrizzia Milo,
the Humble One

I want to close out the noise, to rise above the noise;
the noise that interrupts, that separates,
the noise that isolates.
I want to listen to God again.

www.jesuit.ie/prayer
"Sacred Space"

Contents

A Reflection

In early morning the Sonoran Desert welcomes, the arms of its saguaro cacti stretched wide against blue sky as though to enfold you in their warmth. From a distance the desert seems hospitable, its limitless horizons inspiring both Native Americans and those who came later to broaden their own. Its open heart makes feeling connections to a God or gods and to all that lives effortless. No wonder its native peoples felt at home in this universe. No wonder the desperate and ambitious continue to press their way west.

In the last light of evening, however, the saguaros look like crosses ready for the next crucifixion, spines set to nail the victim and hold him helpless and bleeding. They warn you not to enter unless you are willing to feel lonely and afraid and vulnerable, at least until your hidden strengths have time to emerge. This view of the desert has drawn spiritual explorers for the countless centuries we humans have sought the divine in nature and in ourselves. It is the desert of tribal elders, mystics, and seers, of Mohammed, Moses, and Christ.

The desert's stillness let me finally hear my own voice and occasionally what I thought to be God's.

Both views of the desert live in me and hold sway at different times. I am not sure which moved me to call Desert House of Prayer outside Cortaro, Arizona, to ask whether they had room for me, but I called and they did. This simple act led me to let go of my job and leave my home and children to live in silence there for a time during the longest and hottest days of the desert year. The desert's strong light illuminated my darkest corners and let me see what I had refused to see. The desert's stillness let me finally hear my own voice and occasionally what I thought to be God's. And within it I came to feel connected to all those in the past who had sought the desert's isolation.

Isolation is to be found here, but not escape. While the desert offers a place to be away from other people and outside influences, it is not a place to avoid danger or engagement or thinking. Those who seek to avoid challenge would not find refuge here, but for those about to face major life challenges, the desert can be a crucible. The desert is a good place to hone one's soul for further conflict in the world. It is a good place to cultivate mindfulness, but a poor one to enjoy mindlessness.

The desert does not tolerate pretense or prettiness. Its hard realities make the upkeep of life-lies difficult. So it is a good place to let go of artifice and display. They are useless here and even dangerous. To do well here, you must know what you know. You must accept your limitations or at least be willing to find out what they are.

When I committed to my time at Desert House, I wasn't thinking of the extraordinary experiences of ascetics and monks nor did I aspire to have them. I wasn't thinking at all, just feeling a strong impulse to go there to find answers to questions I had yet to form.

The slice of the Sonoran I chose to retreat to is sometimes called high desert because it is higher above sea level than places like the Sahara or Kalahari deserts. Because high desert allows more vegetation to take hold and the cacti are denser and the pale green paloverde trees sprout everywhere, it is sometimes called green desert. For me it was green, with all the reverberations of hope and new life that color holds.

Day One / Saturday

No Hunting Except for Peace

A van romantically named the Arizona Stagecoach picks me up at the Tucson International Airport, along with some Tucsonites returning home and a divorced dad visiting his son. Our driver could have been a real stagecoach driver. He has the sunbaked skin, blue-sky eyes, and bad teeth I'd want to see cast in the role if I were the director of the film. The dry, western, man-of-few-words humor, too, of which I think he is quite conscious.

He knows he's part of the entertainment and plays out his part more than competently, calls me "little lady." At five feet eight I am hardly little, but I like trying on the role of lady. I am already wearing a broad-brimmed straw hat with a lavender silk band and pale, pink flowers so it's easy to add the rest — the polite flirtation, conscious manners, and acceptance of help that isn't truly needed. I don't protest the adjustment of the sun visor, the moveable stairstep, or the proffered hand upon exit. It all makes me feel fresh, like a new person. I am tired of being me and want to be someone else. Out here in the desert I am.

Who I had been was executive creative director of the Chicago office of J. Walter Thompson, one of the world's largest advertising agencies. I loved my job and its attendant perks until it started to inhabit every space in my head and every hour of my day. I lost the ability to draw boundaries, even when they affected my health or my family. When I had pneumonia I only took one day off and then came in to do an interview with *Adweek* magazine because I thought it would be good for attracting new business. I was sleeping less than five hours a night. I saw my children two hours a day. During the last year, there were only three weekends I didn't work. I was no longer a person, just a position on a hierarchy chart. I felt like an unwatered plant.

Cracks and fissures developed in my personality and my performance. Eventually I could no longer ignore my unhappiness. On a flight back from a new business pitch, I read a book about sabbaticals and was taken with its description of Desert House. Especially the line "Desert House seeks out those who wish to avoid being sought out." Once I booked my stay there, I scheduled a lunch with my boss to tell him I wanted to take time off. He said it was good that I wanted to leave the agency because he'd decided to fire me. I realized that's what I'd wanted him to do for the last six months because I had lacked the courage to just quit. Now I was free not only from my job but from second-guessing my decision to leave. I was going forward full-speed into retreat. Into two weeks of silence.

The Desert House of Prayer is pretty far northwest of town. Including the other dropoffs, it takes us nearly an hour and a half to get there from the airport. I'm glad it seems far. On a retreat you should be far from other people. As the houses, the casitas, the ranches, and the strip malls grow farther and farther apart, I get more and more excited. As we cross railroad tracks in an open area near the turn to Picture Rocks Road, I see what I think is a short, fat tornado.

"Dust devil," Clint says.

My first encounter with a devil in the desert. I see a few more devils before we reach the retreat house cutoff, along with an ominous sign: DO NOT ENTER WHEN FLOODED. I ask Clint why there are warnings since it's so dry.

"See how this road dips down? We're going lower and lower to below sea level. See those mountains over there and up ahead? They may be foothills, but they are damned high. Five thousand feet. Even a short rain can send water racing down those hills and canyons — we call them arroyos — at really high speeds. Before you know it, there can be a wall of water that washes out this road and takes a car or two with it. It's happened before. And the rainy season starts on or about June 30. How long you staying?"

"Till the twenty-eighth, I think."

"Well, you probably won't see any rain. Too bad."

I pray for rain. I want to see it wash out the road. I want to be on a desert island.

We slow down to the posted fifteen miles per hour to make the serpentine curves. The small sign for Desert House comes up suddenly. There is a long forked drive and I can't see any buildings yet. On the fork marked as the entrance is another sign: NO HUNTING EXCEPT FOR PEACE.

About a quarter mile on the right is a small chapel and then dead ahead lie the long, low buildings, all a sun-bleached pale green that blends in with the vegetation.

There are a few trailers to the side with dark green wooden stairs and decks leading up to them that I take to be part of the encampment. It isn't an impressive layout. Because the brochure they'd sent me indicated a library of more than fifty thousand volumes, I expected adobe and brick, something more religious and institutional looking. Something more permanent, historical, uplifting, beautiful. This is rough and poor, unaesthetic. It looks like the kind of setup real estate developers erect as headquarters for new parcels of land they intend to hawk.

After my disappointment comes illumination. This retreat campus is the perfect setting for starting a new life. It is the headquarters for new development I will do within myself. The buildings are unobtrusive and dismissable because they are not meant to dominate either the inner landscape or the saguaros and sagebrush that surround them. They are as transitional as their guests and offer the chance to detach from the world rather than form attachment to a new place within it.

I feel happy. Clint unloads my one lonely piece of luggage from the back of the stagecoach, and I pay him and say good-bye. Then he says he has a present for me, or rather for my daughter.

"Do you know what a pocket rock is?" he asks.

"No," I confess uncomfortably. I always feel anxious when I don't know an answer no matter how innocent or unimportant the question.

"Well, whenever I have time between pickups I stop in the desert to look for them. Remember when we dropped off that older couple? Right in their front yard I found a new one, all smooth and black and small." He smiles, reaches into the pocket of his shirt, and pulls it out. "Small enough to fit in my pocket. Hence the term." He hands the little rock to me.

"I remembered you said your daughter collected rocks, and a pocket rock would be the perfect souvenir for her."

I laugh. "Thank you, Clint."

"See you in two weeks. We'll see if you're any different after your experience. Maybe I won't recognize you. You might cut off your hair and become a nun."

Clint rides off in the appropriate cloud of dust. The sun wasn't setting quite yet so I couldn't say "sunset," but his departure had the same effect. It was classic western.

Nobody came out to meet me, and nobody was to be seen near any of the buildings. Probably the heat. It's ninety-eight degrees at four o'clock in the afternoon, and no one but a snake or a stranger would be out now.

I close my eyes against the light and hear a sweet voice.

The voice introduces itself as Trudy. She will take me to my room and get me settled in. She isn't a nun or a professed religious but a volunteer who lives in Tucson proper most of the time. Right now she lives on the grounds in one of the trailers. "Philip," she calls it. I wonder what she's talking about but soon discover that each room or hermitage, which is what the trailers are called, is named for a different saint. Philip refers to St. Philip Neri. There are cells and hermitages named for Thomas Merton, St. Sophia, John Patmos, Charles de Foucauld, Juan de la Cruz, St. Catherine of Siena, Dorothy Day, and others associated with contemplative life and desert spirituality. There is also a tiny house called "Bede Griffiths," which is isolated from the rest of the campus.

This retreat campus is the perfect setting for starting a new life.

Trudy is small and slim and very fast. Her voice smiles just as her face constantly does. Her short-cropped curly white hair makes her skin look tanner by contrast. She wears big baggy shorts and an open-collar camp shirt in resort colors: aqua, peach, and dusty rose.

She pulls my roller suitcase over bleached-white sidewalk, gravel, and stones to the first building west of the main office. We stop in front of sliding screen and glass doors with a small square of cement patio in front occupied by a white plastic chair. Next to the chair is a large can of Kilz primer that serves as a makeshift table.

"This is Thomas," Trudy says introducing me to my new home. Inside a plaque on the wall says this cell is dedicated to Thomas Merton. It has a tile floor with a few rag rugs, a twin bed and nightstand, a desk and chair, and a La-Z-Boy recliner with a floor lamp for late night reading. One desert landscape print hangs over the unmade bed.

Trudy hands me a neat pile of folded unmatched sheets and thin, worn towels and points out where the extra pillow and blanket are stored, although it doesn't look likely that I'll need them. She shows me how to work the evaporative cooling system and fan and where the cleaning supplies are stored.

Ah, this was the catch. I'd wondered how Desert House could afford to charge the $29 a day I was paying for my accommodations. Part of it is that each guest, following the principles of a simple life, is responsible for his or her own cleaning: linens, floors, dusting, toilet scrubbing, and mirror polishing. There are no maids or room service. When your stay is finished you are expected to leave your cell spotless for the next retreatant.

Trudy pleasantly rattles off the evening's agenda, which I forget as soon as she finishes. Fortunately, there is a horarium on top of the desk. I look it over.

Trudy had explained that these activities were not obligatory. They were suggestions for stimulation. The schedule is as I choose it to be.

WELCOME TO DESERT HOUSE
HORARIUM

Monday through Thursday

6:00 to 6:55 a.m.	Optional Meditation in Chapel
7:00 to 7:30	Morning Praise and Eucharist
7:30 to 8:30	Breakfast (Silent)
12:00 to 1:00 p.m.	Lunch (Silent)
4:30 to 5:15	Optional Meditation in Chapel
5:20 to 5:40	Vespers
5:40	Dinner in Common. (We talk.)
7:00	Conference, movie, etc.

Friday

7:00 a.m.	Eucharistic Liturgy (No music)
	Friday is the community's Hermit Day. Meals are at regular times, but all are taken in silence. Office and meditation times are left to the individual.

Saturday

	Meals at regular times
6:00 to 6:55 a.m.	Optional Meditation in Chapel
7:00	Morning Prayer (No music)
4:30 to 5:15 p.m.	Optional Meditation in Chapel
5:20	Vespers
7:30 p.m. to 7:00 a.m.	Vigil Mass and Adoration of the Blessed Sacrament. Optional Hourly Adoration in Blessed Sacrament Chapel.

Sunday

5:00 to 8:15 a.m.	Breakfast (Silent)
9:00	Morning Praise and Eucharist
11:30 to 12:30	Lunch (Silent)
4:30 p.m.	Vespers and Social Hour
5:20	Dinner in Common (We talk)
7:30	Music Hour

So many choices. To fill the vast open vistas of time that appear between scheduled activities, like plains between mountain ranges, may take more thought and discipline than I can currently muster. Will my afternoons feel like a drive across Nebraska? What will I do with so much time? I can't pray every minute. I don't want to think too much about the past. I don't want to be cooped up in my cell hunched over this desk writing and reading. Would that be any way to enjoy my first days of freedom?

Freedom seems less entrancing now that I consider its attendant responsibility. Conscious decisions are much more demanding than unthinking adherence to The Schedule. In my old life all I had to do was consult my agenda to know what I would do next. Now I will have to examine a nearly infinite array of possibilities.

Not entirely infinite. I look around my cell. How poor Thomas is. No computer, no television. There are only two things in my cell that resemble screens: the big rectangular window and the small square bathroom mirror. Can either bear much watching?

Thomas holds no radio or CD player either. There will be no soothing hum of background music, no beat to draw away nervous energy unless I can harness some from the music of the universe.

There is also no phone. The literature said as much, and I understood that to be positive because that meant no incessant ringing, no requests, no interruptions. Now I think about outgoing calls. What if I get sick or hurt? How will I let someone know? What if I miss my children? What if I want to order a pizza?

I turn the spigot that shuts off the flow of my ever-present stream of meaningless worries. And they do stop. This is too magnificent an opportunity to waste with such banalities. The larger concern is how I will cope with the solitude. The horarium suggests not only unfilled hours but absolute quiet throughout the day. Quiet from seven in the evening until six the next when dinner is taken. Quiet from Thursday evening until Saturday's dinner because Friday is Hermit Day. However, if I choose to attend the traditional prayer services there is at least the promise of melody and lyric, the comfort of harmony, and the pleasure of contributing my own small part to it. Who doesn't love the sound of her own voice?

I decide to attend most of the services, at least for the first few days. It's too soon for me to cut all ties to daily rhythms. There is solace in structure. It's something to bump up against.

I still have forty-five minutes until Vespers, which goes by quickly as I settle my things into their new home. I wonder whether my cell's namesake, Thomas Merton, will influence my thoughts and dreams during my time here. Thomas Merton was a Trappist monk and a prolific writer who had a special appreciation for silence and contemplative prayer. I wonder whether achieving silence was difficult for him, since he was such an intellectually gifted and verbal person. How hard it must have been for him to quiet the cacophony of thoughts in his own head even in the midst of seeming quiet. I ask him to help me reach that level of quiet communion with God he so longed to achieve.

At a quarter past five I walk to Vespers at the Chapel of Our Lady of Solitude. The sun to my skin is like a jalapeño to the tongue. It's still nearly one hundred degrees.

The chapel has a simple spire but few of the other exterior trappings that transport me to a state of awe. There are contemporary stained-glass windows at intervals, but most windows are plain so they can easily open to capture any desert breeze. Behind the altar is a huge picture window, the kind you find in suburban ranch house living rooms, but the scene it frames lifts it beyond the mundane.

The frame holds a single red-flowering saguaro in focus, with mesquite, creosote, bishop's hat, and nearly every kind of desert plant as the background, along with a soft purple mountain range, desert songbirds, and lizards and tiny ground squirrels darting in and out. It is magnificent and makes the space feel holy, filled with God as artist and friend of the weird. I long to look through the window at dawn or at moonrise.

There are two rows of folding chairs facing each other on either side of the altar, which is a large simple table carved from a redwood tree. I am too shy to sit in these seats since they seem to demand sittees who will actively participate in the service, and I don't know enough about it to decide whether I am willing. The regulars like Father Kane, spiritual director of Desert House, Trudy, and what I take to be other staff members, take these chairs. There are others, like me, who hang back and take seats in the folding chairs that face the altar as though it were a stage. We are the audience, those who watch, and we are as necessary to the services as the cantor, the readers, the singers, the confident ones.

We sing psalms. I sing, too: the melodies are not hard to follow and my side of the chapel needs more power as we sing in answer to each other.

After Vespers we head for the dining room without conversation. It is a comfortable silence that actually eases whatever tension might exist when making small talk with strangers. There is a long wooden table set with lit candles, stoneware, and linens in a southwestern motif and a small floral centerpiece. Lillian, one of the lay volunteers, leads grace. It is a prayer she's composed to thank God for the safe arrival of new guests and the safe departure of Sister Gen, who has fulfilled her agreed upon stay as a staffer at Desert House and will now go elsewhere.

As soon as Lillian finishes grace the table erupts in conversation, the words flowing like lava kept under pressure too long. Since I am new and still searching for silence, I find this sudden outflow of words violating. But this is a talking dinner as the schedule forewarned, and the other guests who've been here longer than the few hours I have clearly find their exchanges releasing. They've been silent since Thursday night's dinner — a full forty-eight hours. I don't feel talkative just yet, so I don't volunteer anything. But everyone else offers a piece of her day (there are only three men among the twelve of us) in hope of some reciprocation.

This *is* a good chance to learn a bit about the others with whom I will share the silence.

There is Dwight, a seventy-year-old man who is here to write a book about his ride around the circumference of the United States, which he accomplished in his mid-sixties right after his first wife's death. His second wife,

Yvonne, is at Desert House with him. Their behavior toward each other is very honeymoon. They are a reason to want to grow old together.

There is also a nun who looks like my Aunt Dolores and dresses like an artist for a very good reason: she is one. Sister Jeanne Bartholomew works in woodcuts and prints and also teaches art. She is here to get a start on illustrating a book that was written at Desert House a year ago.

My other dinner partners include a shy accountant who is changing careers and wants to be in human resources and a male choir director from San Francisco whose speaking voice is very melodic and loud. The staff is excited to have him for Sunday Mass because he's agreed to give an organ recital after the service. I remember an organ at the rear of the chapel. It is small, but sufficient to fill the space with what promises to be angelic sound.

I don't say much and give only general answers to polite questions as to what led me here. I mention *Six Months Off*, the book about sabbaticals that listed Desert House as an excellent choice. I don't say anything about feeling burned out or cheated of time with my children. Nor do I delve into other guests' deeper motivations or inner lives. I never even meet the people at the other end of the long table. But coming here isn't so much about meeting others as it is about meeting oneself.

After dinner we are expected to clear the table and organize ourselves to do the dishes. There is no automatic dishwasher so everything must be done by hand. The atmosphere is like the one after Thanksgiving in my grandmother's kitchen — lively, with the constant commotion and many questions about where things go and who should do what, giving us clues to each other's personalities.

I find out who is so self-effacing that she has to ask permission to move a platter or wipe a dish. There is one who is so lazy that she holds a towel and moves around but never actually accomplishes a thing and another who can get in and get the job done without ever asking a question at all. I imagine that this close observation is one of the pleasures, or displeasures, of living in a small religious community like a monastery or a convent.

My own predilection is to do what doesn't require too much direction: dry the dishes, a task made especially easy because the dryers do a hand-off to the put-awayers who already know where everything goes.

As soon as the dishes are put to sleep, the lights are dimmed and the voices hush and finally go silent. We are back within ourselves, alone again. Or if we're very lucky, with God.

The pre-sundown light is extraordinary. It is magic hour in the desert. Through the kitchen window I see rabbits stirring in the mesquite. I also spy stone benches to sit on and contemplate the night life. I rush back to my room for a notebook and a pen. Lillian told me there is a Garden of Gethsemane at the back of the property that winds up and down a hill through the cacti; the purple mountains and the reflected light from the sunset will be in the background. My plan is to visit each of the Stations of the Cross and then sit and write at the last Station, the one visible through the kitchen window.

Heading for the first Station, I have to pass a fallow garden surrounded by a fence and one of the trailers. I pass the trailer slowly and watchfully, the way I used to walk by the reputed haunted house in our town. The trailer is very quiet and dark. I'm not sure what the boundaries of the retreat center are and whether strangers live here. Later, I find out it is one of the hermitages; Dwight and Yvonne have been living in it for a year.

As I head for Station Two, I hear what I think is a rattlesnake. I want to see one outside of a zoo, but I have sandals on and am afraid to wander into the brush.

Bushes swoosh and I can hear the scurry of small animals hunting for food or trying to get away from me. As it darkens, the explorer instinct recedes and I get increasingly timid. Instead of spending time in meditation at each Station of the Cross, I hurriedly say a conventional Hail Mary or Our Father and move on.

When I get to my writing bench it is too dark to write but the rabbits are there. They allow me to join them because I keep still and don't try to approach them. After a while they stop keeping one eye on me and go about their business as though I were as harmless as the bench.

I head back for Thomas, my room. I like calling rooms by names, as though they had a spirit all their own. As I walk past other cells many of them darken, like candles snuffed after church services. It's only nine o'clock, and there are neither diversions nor duties with which to occupy myself. I've already finished the book I brought for the plane. I decide to go to bed now, my children's bedtime, so I can get up at five the next morning and journal for an hour or so before breakfast and Morning Eucharist.

I set the clock and undress by candlelight. There are mournful cries from birds whose calls I don't recognize. I close the glass sliding door and the screen and see that there is no lock. As I lie in the narrow bed in the dark I am aware that I have more fears to confront than merely fear of the blank page. I remember the wolves and bears and clowns I thought lived in my closet when I was a child. But somehow I sleep, and well. Maybe because before I drift off, I write my own bedtime prayer to protect me from my personal demons.

Prayer before Sleep

Every night I lie awake
and think of things that might have been.
Worse yet, I think of things that really were.
Dear God, break the grip of the past upon me.
Let my thoughts be for tomorrow.
And may your power turn hopes into plans
and complaints into courage.

Day Two / Sunday

Lost and Found

I wake before the alarm goes off. It's been a productive sleep. I want to write. But instead of a prayer, a poem spills out.

Before I left my old life behind I'd begun writing prayers. Not the kind many pastors, priests, or rabbis would recommend to their congregation but prayers nonetheless. Prayers filled with the dark contemplations and supplications of someone who believes in God, yes, but isn't convinced God is good or even kind in any conventional sense. "Prayers in the dark" was how I thought of them. They were like the prayer I wrote last night. In the dark.

The idea of writing them came to me when I was part of a class called The Artist's Way, a program originally developed by Julia Cameron but now taught by various people around the country. One of our assignments was to write a prayer for the close of a class and read it aloud. I didn't like the assignment and thought of most prayers as sappy, predictable, and flat. But when I began thinking about what I would write, it forced me to confront my most frightening ideas about God.

One of the things I'd talked to friends about long before I took that course was my belief that God is an artist, the ultimate and original creative person, with all of the good and bad aspects that idea suggests. I feel that since humans are created in God's image we can take the personal characteristics of great artists as our basis for knowing God. You could then posit that God creates for personal pleasure and fulfillment, not for the sake of the created. This God is experimental and believes aesthetics are everything. This God is more amoral than moral, highly sensitive, easily offended or angered, yet paradoxically completely empathetic.

I wrote a prayer directed to this Artist God and read it at my appointed time to the class.

An Artist's Prayer

My God, dear God, oh God.
How often I say your name in vain. In pain. In anger.
Tonight I raise my voice to you in praise.
For you have made a wondrous creature: me.
You made me in your image and likeness.

You like me because I am, like you, an artist.
Together we will keep creating the world
as we want it to be. I am the brush in your hand,
the pen to your page, the flesh of your words.
As I write or type or paint or sculpt
I re-create your majesty, and so myself.
Tonight I say your name and ask for nothing
for you have given me your power to do all.

I was surprised and honored when nearly everyone in the class asked for a copy of it. It made me start thinking about how few prayers there were for outsiders, people who weren't completely with the program of existing organized religions and maybe never could be. I did some research, found nothing like the prayers I wanted to write, and decided to pursue a book of them.

But this morning in the Sonoran Desert no prayers are sent to me. Instead I send myself to breakfast before Sunday's nine o'clock Morning Praise and Eucharist in the chapel.

This is a silent retreat, but it is not the silence of the deaf. With the constant vocal track of everyday chitchat dropped out, the world offers a fresh new mix of melodic lines sung by desert birds, surprising tympani from pots and pans and garbage cans, splashes of water being poured into birdbaths, the scatty scuttle and rustle of people and animals. The quieter it got, the more I could hear. The less I heard of other voices, the more my own emerged. If I could already feel this after a little more than eighteen hours in the compound, what I could feel after days of this silence might well approach the profound.

When I enter the kitchen I am surprised by how sumptuously breakfast presents itself. The bounty is arranged on a long counter: bowls of cantaloupe, honeydew, and kiwi; homebaked wholegrain bread with jams and jellies; cereals, muesli, yogurt, eggs, juices, rolls, cake from last night's dinner. It's like a Sunday brunch. But it will be silent just as all breakfasts and lunches at Desert House are designed to be.

I take breakfast to the end of the long refectory-style kitchen table nearest the window. The window frames a rocky bird grotto where all the desert birds come for their breakfast. It's a companionable and equitable arrangement; they can gawk at us while we eat just as we gape at them while they do. A mother quail leads her babies to the shallow pottery dish for a bath, and like all children they splash a lot. Other birds are perched on the spines of the cholla cacti. We hear their songs because the window is open and no one speaks. I wonder how much natural sound I miss at home because the morning news is blaring or I'm preoccupied with nagging my children to remember their backpacks and brush their teeth.

After breakfast I head for the chapel and take stock of my sins in preparation for receiving Holy Communion. Personal inventory complete, I take stock of the other worshipers. Everyone is dressed up, the women in skirts or dresses, the men in jackets instead of the usual shorts or jeans and hiking gear. There are people in the congregation that I don't recognize from last night's dinner.

A very pretty older woman with a chignon sits next to Father John. She's flamboyant like a tropical parrot, dressed in coral and beautiful bold bracelets and rings with large stones of turquoise and diamond. I find out later that her name is Millie Kaeser and that she is a successful local sculptor whose busts of saints are displayed around this chapel. Her late husband, Fritz Kaeser, was a well-known photographer of the desert who had done several beautiful black-and-white portraits of the artist Georgia O'Keeffe and the photographer Alfred Stieglitz. She was the one who had arranged for a local craftsperson to create the beautiful polished wood altar table.

During the Sign of Peace, the traditional handshake is replaced by warm hugs. I hate public displays of affection, especially with strangers, but it seems more disruptive to deliberately avoid the hugs than to just numb myself and go with the flow. It feels more sincere than I expect it to. All in all, I exchange about twelve hugs with strangers, a lifetime quota.

Although we're supposed to maintain our silence, it's hard to suppress greetings. We greet each other in loud whispers, as though the pretend whispers somehow don't count as real talking. Even Father Kane does it.

I receive communion and for the first time in a long while it is "wet" — emotional instead of rote and dry. The San Francisco choir director gives his promised post-service organ concert, a wonderful tasting of pieces by Bach and Mozart. Mozart is apparently Father Kane's passion. We all gather round the organ as he plays. When he makes a little bow indicating he's finished his performance, we make silent clapping gestures. Our departure is unceremonious. We've exhausted our greetings during the Sign of Peace and give no good-byes as we straggle out separately to face the long silent day.

There's nothing on the schedule until lunch at eleven thirty. I decide to hike on my own. At dinner last night a retreatant who'd been here many times before described a simple trail I could follow on my own. It starts out at the Picture Rocks petroglyphs, winds around a couple of mountains, follows a dry river bed she calls "the

Wash," and then ends up at the abandoned greenhouse near Dwight and Yvonne's trailer.

It's already ninety-five degrees. I fill a bottle with ice water, tuck paper and pen in my pocket in case I'm overcome by inspiration, and set out. I go mapless because I'm sure it will be more fun this way.

What looks dead can be very much alive. The desert outside the Saguaro National Forest looks dead today. Dusty, still brown and brittle green. I look dead. White flaky skin, vacant gray eyes, barely audible voice from a lifetime of too much talking. But the desert and I are both very much alive as I discover in the next two hours.

It's easy to find the Way of the Cross on the hillside, to follow the trail up and around the first mountain. But as the trail goes deeper into the desert and its out-lines become weaker, I can't tell a good path from a bad one. They are all enticing and forbidding at the same time. I yearn to be a pioneer and break new ground, but already I am confronted by my innate unsuitabil-ity for trailblazing. I spend an hour or so wending my way through dry creek beds, precariously piled rocks, echinacea, mesquite, and creosote; sidestepping snake holes; starting at the rustle of lizards, desert quail, and jackrabbits; and avoiding tarantula webs. Soon I'm frus-trated and wish for a well-worn path or the edge of a highway to suddenly appear.

My daydreaming has made me miss the markers I should have been looking for. I am now disoriented and a little scared because I have only a swallow of water left in my bottle.

The heat is getting to me. I feel tired and panicked, can't tell east from west, north from south. All the shapes of the mountains look the same, and as I get closer they seem much taller than they appeared. I clamber up and down the loose stone of one slope only to get to the other side and discover yet another wash and another mountain. It's like climbing the crests of waves that have been frozen in time. My face burns. I'm wearing sunscreen, but now it feels as though my blood is boiling. I stand still and pour the last swallow of water on my scalp. The refreshment calms me down. I sit on a rock and listen for the sounds of cars and trucks on Picture Rocks Road. I hear motors but it's so hard to place where they're coming from.

And then I decide to trust my instincts and walk on. I probably can discover where I am if I would just listen for my own voice as hard as I listened for cars and trucks. Just before I reach the highway I recognize the marker I would have seen if I hadn't spaced out. When I get on the road I realize that I probably walked two miles farther north than I should have and am way past the retreat house or any houses at all. I'd even walked past the box canyon I was told to look for that was the setting for an old dramatic television series called *The High Chapparal*. It is still a few more miles to the main house, but at the top of the next hill I can see clearly where I am and where I'm headed. I slow down and relax. My heart stops pounding.

Back in the cool of Thomas I look in the mirror and see my face is dark red, not from sunburn but from fever. I drink glass after glass of cold water and take a shower. It takes over an hour for my internal furnace to shut itself down.

I feel stupid. None of this would have happened if I'd brought enough water and worn a hat. I pull the unused pen and paper from my pocket and put it on the desk. So much for writing or even thinking. I'd thought the rhythm of walking would set off writing rhythms in my brain that would result in poems and prayers and prose with dream sequence cadence, but all I'd experienced was dull panic and ruminating thoughts like "You're lost, you idiot; you're going to die."

I look at my watch. Twelve thirty. I've missed lunch and am very hungry. I run to the kitchen even though it's nearly a hundred degrees out hoping the food hasn't been completely removed. Luckily there are still some sandwich fixings and leftovers available on the buffet.

As I eat and watch the birds I think about how much my hiking decisions are like my life decisions. I start out okay but then impulsively make moves I later regret, moves that deny the existence of danger even when it's obvious. Or I'm making great headway, great time, and then I get bored and wonder whether there is a secret way, a more beautiful path the average person wouldn't take and that I alone would discover. So I veer off. I'd done it with jobs, with relationships, with things as superficial as my hair.

I decide to visit the fifty-thousand-volume library after lunch and spend the afternoon reading in my shaded little cell. It's supposed to get to 106 degrees today. In the library there is a welcome table display-ing lovely coffee table books: the photographer Fritz Kaeser's work, medieval illuminations, a book featur-ing the world's most beautiful retreats. More of Millie's busts are here, too. There are tall cases with many vol-umes by Thomas Merton, Aquinas, the Desert Fathers, biblical scholars, Catholic and Buddhist theologians, and philosophers. There is a very respectable collection of classical and contemporary poetry and fiction.

It makes me feel hungry and parched. I want to check out every volume. It's been so long since I've been able to read, really read, spend a whole afternoon on a book. I check out volumes by Hildegard of Bingen, Merton, Raymond Carver, and Simon Tugwell, a twentieth-century English theologian. I greedily snap up volumes about the Desert Fathers and Mothers. Then I return to Thomas with my cache and settle in to the La-Z-Boy for a long read until Vespers.

I open Simon Tugwell's *Ways of Imperfection* first. His style of writing is dryly funny because it is so direct and unsparing in its incisions into human motivation and rationalization. It's very English.

Tugwell is fond of Julian of Norwich (ca. 1342–ca. 1420), a writer, mystic, and hermit. I am taken with Julian, too, even apart from her having my son's name. I am taken because I take hope from her assessment of sin: "Sin enters into the divine perspective; it is not wasted, because what God wants is precisely saints who have been sinners."

I race through the book, my aforementioned hunger forcing me to gulp rather than digest the material. In my gluttony I next indulge in *The Wisdom of the Desert: Sayings from the Desert Fathers of the Fourth Century* by Thomas Merton. These Desert Fathers were the first Christian hermits. They abandoned the pagan cities to live in silence in their personal quests for salvation, fleeing to the deserts of Egypt, Palestine, Arabia, and Persia. They sought a society where all were equal and the only authority was that of God. They did not believe that the divisions between the powerful and the powerless that resulted from secular societies were just. They rejected the false self required by life in the secular world in favor of a true self they felt they could only find in Christ. But for hermits who shunned conversation they certainly had a great deal to say. They valued love over all other practices of spiritual life, even contemplation, solitude, and prayer. To love as they considered ideal was to let go of anger and entitlement. Many of them never achieved the state of perfect love they envisioned. They were human. I take heart from the stories of their failures and from their determination to do better next time. They knew they were sinners and didn't consider themselves holy men. They weren't the least bit judgmental. Abbot Moses said, "My own sins are running out like this sand," as he let sand sieve through a basket with many holes, "and yet I come to judge the sins of another." Merton says that Abbot Antony of Egypt, considered the Father of Desert Fathers, got to a point where he thought even the devil must have some good in him because he was created by God.

There were Desert Mothers as well as Desert Fathers, although Merton touched only briefly upon them and quoted only Abbess Syncletica. One of them, Macrina the Younger, a sister of Gregory of Nyssa, founded a convent on her family's estate in Cappadocia in the fourth century. These women also held strong convictions about the superiority of love and the virtues of monasticism. Several ascetic communities of women predated those of their male counterparts. Some of these women were dubbed "harlots of the desert" because they had originally pursued monks to tempt them. But they were then overcome by the monks' holiness and withdrew into convents to seek divine forgiveness and the greater beauty of God. I decide to do further reading on them during my stay.

As I immerse myself in the sayings of the Desert Fathers I become very interested in the hermits' efforts to overcome anger because I am so often in its grip myself. My anger arises so quickly that it doesn't even feel that I've decided to be angry; I just am. I struggle with counting to ten and the other prescribed cooldown techniques but am usually unsuccessful. This makes me wonder whether I'm secretly arrogant. But if I am, why am I so reticent to assert power, so reluctant to stay in the spotlight for long, hesitant to say "no" to others' demands no matter how difficult they might be? Maybe in my arrogance I don't want to be seen as unable to bear a heavier load. I don't want to be one of the lesser ones, the weak of will. That's why it took me so long to let go of my job. I didn't want to admit I wasn't strong enough to withstand its demands.

Abbot Macarius said that "if, wishing to correct another you are moved to anger, you gratify your own passion. Do not lose yourself in order to save another." Abbot Ammonas, a fifth-century monk of northern Egypt, said that he spent fourteen years praying to God to be delivered from anger. And Abbot Agatho said that even if an angry man were to revive the dead he would not please God because of his anger.

Their warnings are what I need to hear. By 4:25 I am on the last page, just in time to leave for Vespers.

Because it is Sunday a social hour will follow Vespers, complete with wine, scotch, and sherry. Millie Kaeser, the sculptor, is with us this evening, and she holds forth on her memories of John Kane and the birth of Desert House and the pleasure she and her husband took from their visits here. I only hear bits and pieces because tonight it is a full house and I am half a room away.

There is a new retreatant with us as well, Sister Rosina, who is ninety. She is like tissue paper, nearly transparent because her skin has become so thin and white.

Sister Rosina wears a small veil in her pouf of white curly hair. Her eyes are rosary bead blue, like the gemstone aquamarine, and though they technically are seeing less and less they seem to see more and more. She is aware of everyone in the room and aware of their perception of her. She has the crowd instincts of a born entertainer and quickly captures the stage from Millie. Rosina says she isn't ninety but nineteen and that she plays the piano. Her job at the convent is to play the piano in the lobby to welcome visitors. She wants to play for us but the retreat house lacks a piano.

Lillian rings the bell to call us to dinner. Rina, the cook, has made something special from her repertoire, and the scent wafting from the kitchen is direct from *Like Water for Chocolate.* It's chicken mole. Our grace this evening thanks God for the presence of such precious guests as Millie and Rosina, and asks for safe travel for Sister Genny, who will be returning later this evening.

There is more wine at dinner, cleanup, and then once again the luxury of silence. It is seven o'clock. There are no phones visible in either the cells or common rooms so I decide to walk the mile or so to the nearest outdoor public phone. I should let my husband and children know I'm okay. As I start down the road past the chapel I notice the smell of rot and death in the air. As I walk it gets stronger. The closest smell I can think of is that of rotting, moldy pumpkins in November when they've overstayed their Halloween welcome. It turns out to be a dying saguaro, one that is probably close to 150 years old. It is bent over at the top where its spines have become weak and dry and the fibers are separating the way the inside of a spaghetti squash does when you take a fork to it. Parts of it have become blackened, and there are bugs feasting on the exposed innards. With the sun falling lower in the sky behind it, the cactus silhouette with its dark arms and bent head is as sad as the dying Christ on a crucifix.

It makes me melancholy. I walk faster to the phone. Hearing Fabiana's, Viveca's, and Julian's voices is revitalizing but painful. I'm not going to see them for a while.

Because I miss them I make noises to my husband, Jim, about cutting short my retreat. He says he wants me to stay because he's finally getting attention from the kids. I'm jealous, but he's right. I hog them whenever I am home. I said that not reading made me hungry for books, but it is equally true that working such long hours in the advertising business has made me ravenous for my own children. Before I set off for the desert, I was at home with them for two weeks without distraction. They were my meditation. I stared at Fabiana so much that it made her uncomfortable. "Stop looking at me, mama," she complained. But I could tell that she liked my preoccupation with her every word and action. So why have I left them again so soon? Because I will be better for them if I get myself centered and once again in communion with God.

Back at Thomas I sit in the little white plastic chair on the two-foot-square patio and enjoy a cold glass of water. The sun is setting on my first full day. I spend the remaining few hours praying and writing. I think again of the Desert Fathers and their lessons about anger.

Prayer to a Once Angry God

Through nearly all the Old Testament
You were angry all the time.
Like me you had to
get in the last word,
exact vengeance, win.
Then you changed.
In the New Testament
you loved, forgave,
turned the other cheek.
This is why I ask you now
to help me do the same.
Shut my eyes
to new offenses.
Stop my tongue before it lashes out.
Turn anger to love
as you turned water to wine.
Change me
as you once changed yourself.

Day Three / Monday

Sun and Moon

I wake as soon as the sun comes up. When I look at the clock it is 5:15, five minutes before the alarm would have gone off. I like waking up unmechanically to light and birds and quiet.

My vow is to journal the rest of the time I'm here. Journaling the way Julia Cameron recommends it — a straight unedited stream of consciousness. It doesn't guarantee literature, but it often results in truth.

My first jotting is of a dream I had last night that is very threatening but doesn't make much sense. It is peopled by friends and acquaintances who've taken on more sinister roles — not toward me, but toward each other. Brain toxins are being released as I sleep, the cleansing effect of retreat. As I set down the last of my baffling dream the clock says six. It's time for morning meditation.

I take a chair in one of the two rows near the altar and remove my shoes as I see the others do. At exactly six,

Trudy rings a set of handbells once, triggering everyone to rise. Then, in unison, all bow from the waist toward each other, turn and lift their chairs, and face them outward toward the windows. On second bells, we sit.

For the next twenty minutes there is absolute stillness as we retreat into our inner worlds silently repeating our personal mantras. It is important to choose the right one. I spend the first five minutes of the session leveling harsh judgments on the various mantras that suggest themselves to me, not unnatural for a former creative director, and finally settle on: "The words will come to me."

I find it hard to concentrate, hard not to drift to other places and times. I think about the mantra Robert the Reader, a psychic I'd once consulted, had given me long ago: "I am love waiting to be found." Although it seemed silly I was lonely enough then to try it. Less than six months later I fell in love with the man I eventually married. So I can't easily dismiss mantra power.

After twenty minutes, Trudy rings the handbells once more, and we rise and turn to our right. Then Trudy leads us in a slow rhythmic procession around the chapel and back to our seats. Once again the bells signal us to return to meditation.

It's easier to concentrate during the second twenty minutes now that I've chosen not the perfect mantra but a serviceable one and stopped the critic in my soul. It seems only a moment later when the bells ring again. All rise and bow to each other. We readjust our chairs, put on our shoes, and then resettle for Morning Praise and Eucharist.

We sing a psalm, and I realize how much I miss singing and church music. It brings me back to my childhood, when I went to Mass three times a week and often accompanied my Grandma Sally to novenas and vigils. Does the beauty of the ritual lead to a deeper faith, or is it faith that creates such beauty? The flicker of blue vigil lights, the smell of frankincense, the song of the bells — all of these make me feel closer to God. Such beauty could find its impulse only in him. Or her. I find myself defaulting to "him" from childhood habit even though I believe strongly that God is both feminine and masculine. I go back and forth between "he" and "she" in my written prayers, unable to resolve the issue neatly. I recently read that early Christians believed so, too. Many of them thought the Trinity's Holy Spirit represented God's feminine side.

After Mass and silent breakfast I break the pledge of silence and quietly ask Kate, the guest from California who knows all the trails through the mountains, to guide me on a hike this morning. She agrees.

Kate carries a large walking stick and says I should. It's not so much for walking as it is a defensive weapon in case we should encounter a snake sleeping in the sun in the wash or on a warm rock on the trail. I realize what chances I've been taking, daydreaming instead of observing while I hike, thereby turning myself into snake bait.

Kate also carries much more water than I do. On the other hand, she doesn't wear any sunscreen. "Don't believe in it" she says dismissively, as though sunscreen were a religious issue. What Kate believes in is the power of sweat to rid your body of toxins and heavy metals. She has been diagnosed as suffering from heavy metal poisoning, and it has affected her joints, her asthma, her personality. She comes to Desert House to free her body of toxicity and free her spirit of anger about the toxicity.

We start out briskly, making our way through a small winding brush trail that widens when it reaches a big outcropping of rocks that resemble cliffs. At first I don't notice the designs on their face because the drawings are pale and the sun is bright, but these are the famed Picture Rocks that act as canvas for Native American petroglyphs dating back several hundred years. There are pictures of men and women going about their gathering and hunting and lines of ungendered people with joined hands that look like the lines of paper doll cutouts children make in primary school art classes. There are also coyotes and animals with horns that might be rams. The petroglyphs are yellow, and their color is enhanced by the yellow wildflowers that look like paper flowers or whispering bells peeking through the rock face crevices.

While the origin of the petroglyphs isn't certain, they are thought to have been made by Hohokam tribe members who farmed and hunted in the area several hundred years ago. When I later try to track more information I am unsuccessful in pinpointing a date but discover that the Hopi also created similar petroglyphs. One of several reasons such drawings were made might be to mark that they had lived in a particular place just before they left the area for one with richer soil or better hunting. The petroglyphs are a wordless history, perfect for a place that is now the locus for seekers of silence. And they have created a sacred space around them.

Kate asks me whether I can see the big clock-like circle painted on one of the higher rocks. I can. At its center is the startpoint of a spiral that winds out to the edges of the circle. She says she was here when it illuminated on the summer solstice a few years back. I don't understand what she means so she educates me.

"On June 21, the first day of summer, starting at about eleven in the morning, you see a spot of bright light appear where the six would be on a clock. As time draws closer to noon, the light follows the hours up the clock until at noon, bright light illuminates the twelve mark and forms a dazzling pyramid of light right below it on the clock's center line. As time moves past twelve, the triangle grows fainter and then all points of light disappear. It's so powerful. I wish you could see it."

We share quiet smiles when we realize simultaneously that we will both be at Desert House for this year's solstice. I feel privileged to be let in on this historic and nearly mystical experience. As we resume our hike I think about how central the sun is in so many belief systems. The Egyptians built their mythology around the sun; Ra was the sun god. Japan is the Rising Sun. Ancient Norse rites celebrated the sun and the fertility it made possible. The Land of the Midnight Sun is still an honorific. In modern times we worship the sun by heading for it in winter and by basking in it until we tan if we're ungraced by darker skin. This despite warnings about how lethal its rays can be.

America's indigenous peoples celebrated the sun's beneficence in delivering them from darkness as one would hope any god worthy of the name could do.

The solstice picture also functioned as a yearly calendar mark much like an ordinary sundial does for each day. It was a practical way to mark the longest day of the year and the beginning of the most valuable growth period for crops. It was also homage, a beautiful portrait painted of the sun, the most important being in the universe. Picture Rocks was a Hohokam art gallery that displayed some of their most important work. I can't wait to see the sun portrait at its maximum beauty next week. Kate leads me through a different part of the wash and over a hill I haven't crossed before. We stop at its top and she asks whether I can see the windmill. I can't. I'm not used to looking for things outside. When she impatiently says, "Right there!" I still can't see it. My husband says I have no peripheral vision, not because I have any eye problems but because my mental focus is so intense I don't see anything but the central object. Kate gives up on me and we walk on.

Then when I'm not really looking for it I suddenly do see the mill's paddles turning in the wind, pumping water to the surface. It is much smaller than I expected. When I give up on seeing what I expect, I find what I want to see. Up close the sound of the water seems magical, coming as it does in the middle of all this dust and stone and dryness. I walk around back of the windmill to the water trough and see that hundreds of bees have found their oasis and won't give up their basking places readily. We decide to move on.

As we round another mountain, I ask whether the black stony ground is the lava of a now dormant volcano. Kate says it's more likely a souvenir from coal mines that used to operate out here before the turn of the century. We are probably walking the coal roads the miners used to haul away their day's work. Now the black crystals seem a blight on the landscape instead of a key to the area's geological past. I imagine the coal miners making their way up and down these mountains, so deceptively difficult to traverse, to make a paltry day's wage. On the other hand I'm now huffing and puffing up and around them for free just for the promise of a few psychic rewards, a bit of silence, and healthy exercise. The hike seems so easy, the path so clear as I walk it with Kate. Some people have a gift for seeing paths. I don't and I wish I did. Kate never questions her choices, reads without ambiguity the markers other hikers have left, and leaves considerate new markers of her own for me and unknown other retreatants who will take these paths looking for God or peace or both.

We're about two hours into our hike when we run out of water. It's not dangerous because we can see our destination less than a thirty or forty-minute walk ahead, but my face burns pepperhot again. Silence makes the heat more bearable and keeps our supply of saliva from running out.

Luckily there's water at a tiny unmarked bookstore associated with another retreat center on the other side of Picture Rocks. We stop there for a silent drink before heading back to our cells. The bookstore sells some simple spiritual aids. I pick up a crystal rosary in a blue the color of my eyes — light and clear like I want my soul to be. I'm not sure I remember how to pray the rosary so I buy an instruction pamphlet for a quarter. I also buy guardian angel pins for my children. I'm a classic spiritual tourist but unashamed. I'm sure the Good Wife of Bath brought back something with her, too.

Back at Thomas I consult Dom Hubert von Zeller: "Boredom is material for prayer. Loneliness and the inability to find peace in solitude are very much the material for prayer. Restlessness, lack of outlet, waste of natural gift, stagnation and sterility: these are not only subjects for prayer but dispositions for prayer; faith is not always recognizably heroic."

I feel these words were meant to inspire me, to encourage me in my plan to write a book of unusual prayers, and so I take a sidetrip from my reading to brainstorm a list of possible titles.

Resuming my afternoon with Dom Von Zeller, I find other passages of interest. "When God sends us crowded days, it is because he wants us to find our prayer in our work rather than in solitude."

What if God sends you nothing but crowded days for ten years? That's what I feel I've lived through. A blur of births and deaths and promotions and setbacks, bottles and diapers, birthdays and anniversaries, embarrassments and triumphs, and a calendar filled with meetings at fifteen-minute intervals. Was my life with all its makeshift arrangements, delegations, and shirkings really a prayer? Was all this doing without thinking some way of honoring God? I liked the concept of action as prayer, fulfilling the old axiom about actions speaking louder than words. And if I did then in all my whirl of activities actually pray, the next step was to believe I was a prayer. I am God's prayer.

I zip through Von Zeller and everything else I pick up as though it would disappear if I didn't read it whole immediately. In a way, it would. In eleven days I will be back to the joys and responsibilities of parenting, which are always more interesting than all the other options, including gleaning the wisdom of theologians and sages.

This afternoon I have enough time to sample my secular selections. I have Raymond Carver's *Cathedral* at home, but I want to revisit it. He was my teacher for a semester in the MFA program at Goddard College in Vermont, and reading him is a way of connecting with that part of my past, a time when I believed in my own gifts and in anything being possible, with or without God's grace. Because the MFA program was a flexible one for writers with already established careers, I was in Vermont for only four to six weeks a year. So Vermont's piney mountains were a refuge and retreat for me then just as the Sonoran Desert is now. The dorms were simple wooden affairs with a single phone in the kitchen. In the winter we snowshoed to classes through the silent white woods. There is so much spirituality in place.

I remember that Carver had been in advertising, too, but that he'd gotten out earlier than I did. It's hard to be in advertising past the age of forty-five, not because of what aging does to your looks, but because of what it does to your soul. It makes you want to seek the eternal, which puts you directly at odds with a business that worships what's current and hip.

Looking younger is easy now because there are so many "cures": treadmills and trainers; eye surgery, face-lifts and liposuction; wearing black leather clothing and closely cropped hair. And if you've lasted that long in advertising you can usually afford all the options.

Thinking younger is easier now, too, because all of mass culture has become youth culture. Rock is the anthem of all the generations the media cares about so it's almost difficult not to know which groups are hot even if you don't make an effort to listen to their music. Fashion and star-focused magazines and television shows make it easy to keep up with style news and know what to wear to project the right image. Twenty-four-hour news programming makes it easy to know what's happening around the world, not just in your own city. It's all too easy to know what's new. What's much harder is to hang on to some sense of the eternal with so much pressure going the other way. As I grow older I yearn for a time when I will be exempt from all this frenetic keeping up and staying on. I want to slow down, to gain the wisdom that comes only through reflection and contemplation, to form the independent views that flourish when you aren't subjected to the constant buzz of other people's opinions. I want to hear less and know more.

I want to grow old with the world's blessing instead of its horror. No, that's not exactly right. I don't want to grow old as much as I want to become timeless, without generation. Maybe I'm guilty of the hubris of reaching for immortality, but then I'm in good company

60

since most religious and spiritual movements promise some form of eternal life. The Hopi and Hohokam believe that spirit lasted on. The Hindus believe in the eternal life of reincarnation. The secularists promise eternal life through writing books and making art and erecting buildings. Somewhere in the Silicon Valley they're inventing cybersouls to live on ad infinitum or at least as long as their chips are properly serviced. All spiritual disciplines require maintenance and exercise. Those who worship their own bodies as temples know this best of all.

Before I know it afternoon is over. It's time for meditation, but I don't want to go. I want to stay here with my books a while longer, so I skip the Zen meditation and go to Vespers instead.

For dinner, Rina treats us to stuffed poblano peppers and rice and beans. One of my dinner partners lets me in on a secret drink Rina prepares in the blender for good health and weight loss. Because Rina leaves us to cook dinner for her real family as soon as our food is served. I write a note to ask her for this miracle recipe and pin it to the kitchen bulletin board.

The *Arizona Star* says there is to be a full moon tonight, and I want to be outside to capture it with my cheap disposable camera. I always feel keyed up during a full moon, and I have been feeling a caffeine-like buzz. I am pleased to find out that it's just the moon that's making me feel this way and not some new form of anxiety.

I return to Thomas to write and pray before moon-rise.

A Querulous Prayer

Why is it that whatever I ask of you
isn't what you want to give me?
If I ask for love, you give me loneliness.
If I ask for success, you give me setbacks.
If I ask for time to play, you give me more to do.
Is it what I ask or how?
Grant me then the grace
to answer my own prayers.
Let me learn to ask for
what can be granted.

I put down my pen, grab my camera, and set out to make my date with the moon.

The moon does not disappoint. It is bigger than any I have ever witnessed, and very white. It seems to have a sense of its own grandeur and possesses a flair for making an entrance, pausing once it clears the horizon line so that all heads turn to look at it.

I feel as excited as a child, privileged to have been invited to this party and see the celebrity moon. I head for the garden of the Stations of the Cross, thinking it will provide perfect frames for my pictures of this glorious sky. Through the viewfinder I position a cross dead center on the moon and click. Then I snap another frame of the moon behind a giant saguaro and another of the chapel spire against the rosy sky. Because the sun hasn't quite set the few clouds on the horizon radiate a cotton candy pink that makes the moon seem even more ethereal, like a ball in Cirque du Soleil. I become aware that someone else is with me in the garden. Francesca, a new guest who is staying in one of the hermitages. Her face looks as mine must, suffused with joy and excitement. Although we have never spoken, I feel a bond with her. She has also recognized the beauty and importance of this event. I point to the moon and she nods her head enthusiastically. Spontaneously, we both fold our hands in prayer and bow to each other. It's as though we've been to church, to our own private cathedral without walls.

I continue up the Golgotha-like hill, headed for the chapel. I want to see whether the moon is visible through the altar window. There are no lights on in the church, but it is always unlocked so I push open the screen door and enter, pausing for my eyes to adjust to the semi-darkness. There is a chalice at the center of the altar, and the moon is floating above it as though it were a giant host. I know this is a sacred moment and kneel.

I have been let in on a mystery, allowed to see the world as its Creator must, as art and magic.

I return to Thomas and follow the pamphlet's instructions for saying the rosary. It's been thirty years since the last time I've gone through this ritual, and now that I don't have to do it unless I want to it seems much more compelling. In the eighth grade it seemed like one more ridiculous requirement of the Catholic religion. I couldn't imagine how these rote recitals of ancient prayers could possibly please God, the universe's most creative being. Now I choose to spend my vacation time on feeling the power of these ancient words and the connections they forge between me and the citizens of heaven.

I turn off all the lamps and light three candles, turning my room into a private chapel. I raise the windows and let in the heat, opening myself to the world outside my walls. I lie listening to animal squabbles and bush rustling until the candles burn out and I fall asleep.

Day Four / Tuesday

Nurture and Nature

I don't feel like going to meditation. Again. I get a cup of coffee from the kitchen and sit down at my desk to journal.

"Yesterday I saw a saguaro over twenty feet high with five stems. With two of its stems wrapped around its trunk, it seemed to be hugging itself, providing its own comfort. That it could was no doubt the result of good mothering. Seventy-five years of nurturing, I'm told, is what it takes to get a saguaro baby past the dangerous years of early childhood. If it can make it to seventy-five, its life expectancy is nearly two centuries.

"This nurturing is provided by a nurse or mother plant that grows right next to the baby. The mother needn't even be a saguaro and is often a paloverde tree. Mother and child stay together until the mother plant dies. At seventy-five the baby blooms bright white flowers with yellow hearts and then, absorbed in its own beauty or virility, forgets about its long-suffering mother. The saguaro child is now forty feet tall and towers over the mother tree. If she happens to be a saguaro, she has shrunk to only about three feet tall.

"After the mother dies, I think the young tall saguaro misses her, and this is why he wraps his arms around himself, to remind him of her love.

"I wish I had six arms. Eight arms. If I hug myself I have no arms or hands to do anything else and there is so much to do. I have three babies. My mother is still alive and still taller than I am, but her two arms are wrapped around herself in grief at the loss of another child. She cannot help me. I must stand taller, be content with my two busy arms, my daily growth. My children need my shade even more than I need comforting."

There's still time before Morning Prayer and breakfast so I head to the kitchen for a cup of coffee, which I enjoy in a rocker facing the patio off the dining room. The rabbits and blackheaded titmice are scampering out back, oblivious to my voyeurism.

Although I've already looked out this kitchen window several times before, it all looks new again. The mountains reveal organ pipe and saguaro this morning that weren't visible last night.

Maybe nothing is ever the same twice. If so, how can we ever claim we're bored? Ennui, acedia, is an affront to the artist, to the Creator, because in boredom one fails to see the subtleties of the artist's work. Children recognize this when they watch the same video twenty times or more. They see different things every time. They appreciate the fine points of the artistry.

I used to hate the concept of eternity, an endless roll of sunrises and sunsets and facing every task again and again and again like Sisyphus. But here in the desert I think it is a luxurious, indulgent idea. Eternity gives you time to see every scene. The first time the rabbits, the next time the birds, the next time one's self.

I go to Morning Prayer, but all I can think about is breakfast. After the blessing I am the first to leave the chapel and enter the kitchen. Because I am the first one to table, I get to flip the daily meditation card in the center to the correct one for today's date. It says that you can't earn grace or work for it. You simply accept it as a gift, Christ's gift to you. I understand. I had to learn not to work so hard at falling in love. As soon as I stopped looking for love it found me.

Because I am early I catch a chair near the sliding screen doors, a prime bird-watching perch. A curve-billed thrasher's "whit-wheet" intermingles with the soft clack of spoon against cup and apologetic scrape of chair leg against tile as the other retreatants find their own observation points and breakfast nooks. A Gila woodpecker methodically taps a saguaro to make a hole for a nest that another bird, probably an elf owl or a gilded flicker, will call home. A covey of Gambel's quail races in to feed at the newly filled clay dish calling four notes that sound like "chi-ca-go-go." Maybe they are guessing at my habitat and have aptly hit upon my city of origin. Maybe they observe the human feeders even more keenly than we observe them.

There is a near gridlock of birds near the watering dish because the white-winged doves have pulled up. When they drink their fill, they perch on the surrounding saguaros. The doves are credited with cross-pollinating the saguaro's flowers. When they fly the bright whiteness of their wings dazzles, but in repose they are just an ordinary sooty gray with only a ruffly white line to indicate the hidden beauty of their wings.

A grayish green black-chinned hummingbird goes for the nectar in the hummingbird feeder, appearing to stall in midair though its wingbeats are eighty per second. I think it's a male because it sports a tiny flash of violet band on its black throat. As I turn to watch the brown-patterned cactus wrens bathe in the little grotto outside the sliding kitchen doors I feel very lucky. I am rich in time. With no possessions to take care of and nothing to buy but books, I own my day and my soul in a way I haven't felt since childhood. A morning is now endless, the way it used to feel when I was twelve or thirteen in July. A day or even a minute is as long or short as I want it to be.

What a luxury it is to have the time to notice the little things, to study a cactus flower or to feel the energy coursing through a saguaro's veins. What a gift to watch the Gambel's quail family keep its young in line (they have to occasionally resort to screaming and pecking, just like human mothers) and to see how alike all we creatures really are. What indulgence it is to hike to places by instinct and sight without compass or map, knowing that if I get lost I won't be late for an appointment. I might miss Vespers, but that's easily made up through my idle but constant prayer. God always waits for me no matter how late I am. After the twenty-minute grace period afforded by convention, God doesn't leave in a huff. God won't fire me or banish me from the communion of the faithful. And if I desert her I will be welcomed back as warmly as the Prodigal Son. God's arms, like the saguaro's, are always ready to enfold. The Holy Spirit, like the nurse tree, is always there to protect a vulnerable soul.

It is freedom not to be tied to meetings and time sheets, but now I feel a different kind of time pressure, one of using my time wisely, of planning my days perfectly. I have been feeling inklings for the past year that I won't make it through my forty-eighth year, probably because the grandmother whom my middle name honors, Alice, died of a heart attack when she was forty-eight. She was overweight and had diabetes and was in very different condition than I am, but I still can't shake the feeling that the next couple of years are it for me and I'd better make the most of them. For that matter, the next two weeks are probably all the private time I'll have for a long while so I want to make the most of them.

My natural inclination is not to plan at all but just make it up as I go along. This doesn't seem the path to serious accomplishment, however, so I begin listing things I want to do before I leave Desert House. One of them is to have a private meeting with Father John Kane. All guests of Desert House may seek private spiritual guidance from any of the staff. While I like and respect the other staff members, Father John radiates holiness, and he was the founder of this retreat center. I want to get his guidance on further spiritual reading and discuss my prayer book idea with him to see whether it has any merit from the point of view of a dedicated religious. I've been afraid to bother him — even though I know he will agree to see me — because he always looks like he is listening to God, and that's a conversation I don't want to interrupt.

I also want to see more of the geography of Arizona and maybe visit a Spanish mission. And I want to learn more about desert plant and animal life, a part of this new desire to see the little things. Like the line between prayer and poetry, the line between poetry and science also seems very thin.

Enough of thinking, of living in my head. I go back to Thomas, grab my gear, and set out to find the windmill on my own. It's time to gather some primary knowledge: firsthand experience, no secondary or tertiary resources. No books. Hiking is undiluted, unscreened, unabridged, unedited. Un. That's what I want. At least for a few hours.

When I reach the windmill I watch the bees cover the surface of the water trough like a glistening bejeweled carpet. I never knew bees were drawn to water, but here they are gathered like beachgoers trying to escape a heat wave. Now that I have the time I see not only bees but birds, birds everywhere. I note their markings, and when I return from my wanderings I go straight to *Birds of North America* to look them up: glossy black phainopepla, yellow-breasted warbler, the turkey vulture with its bare, inflamed red head. I note the chubby black-throated sparrows, much cuter than the common sparrows back in Illinois, the red-streaked finches, and the yellow-breasted orioles. I haven't seen a roadrunner yet but really want to even if it doesn't "beep-beep" as in the cartoons. At home I can't get much past robins, sparrows, and cardinals even though the skies and trees are just as thick with different species there as they are here. I just don't see them as I rush to load the kids in the minivan for their trip to school and my trek downtown. My daughter Viveca can recognize almost any bird or animal and explain in detail its habits and preferences, but she is still living in child-time.

Every year the name of the species of tree that looms over our front lawn escapes me. (A linden.) But here I can spot mesquite, creosote, echinacea, the fleshy but spiny green pads of the opuntia and lemon yellow buck-horn cholla that look like vigilant bucks stopping to survey their surroundings. I spy devil cholla spreading across the desert like groundcover, big-padded beavertail with impossibly pink blooms, bluish purple Santa Rita cholla with yellow flowers, prickly pear, bishop's hat, paloverde, imported Texas laurel, cane cactus. I learned that the scarlet flower of the saguaro at the center of the chapel window is actually its red fruit, but I am consoled that almost everyone thinks it is a red flower. (The saguaro's flowers are actually white with a bright yellow center.)

I am a beginner again. A beginner who isn't afraid to be seen as such, who sees the wonder in all. I am student, tourist, child. It seems almost a shame to pass through this state and go on to mastery. Maybe that's why I never really let myself feel my expertise as an advertising professional or a mother. I like everything to seem new all the time.

After ninety minutes of hiking I am lost again. Since I am lost in the very same place I was a few days ago, a better way to think of it is that I found myself in the very same place I had been lost. There is something about these hikes that is a lot like the movie *Groundhog Day.* I'm going to keep doing them over and over again until I get them right. It reminds me of when I used to throw the I Ching. I began to believe in the method's power to pick up my vibrations when I asked the same question three times, and the three silver dimes I threw ended up in the same exact calligraphic figure every time! This when the possible combinations were sixty-four. Sometimes the universe *is* trying to tell you something.

I'm not afraid to be lost this time. I'm embarrassed at my own unmindful stupidity but laugh at the black humor of my predicament. I know I'll be able to wend my way out eventually. And I do — an hour later.

After a shower I head once again for the library, a landscape I can navigate without getting lost except in reverie. I still have a couple of books in my room, but I want my bookcase to be full of choices, to have right in front of me the perfect material for whatever my mood or inclination might be.

I pick up a thick paperback volume of Annie Dillard's *Collected Works,* a volume of Hildegard of Bingen's, and *Letting Go of Shame.* It's ironic that I have come to a Catholic retreat center thinking it will rid me of shame and guilt. But maybe it does in a hair-of-the-dog way, like having a beer with a shot of tomato juice to cure a nasty hangover. Poetry and prayer. The parallels keep clicking for me. To supplement my in-room arsenal of Louise Gluck's *All Hallow's Eve* and *Descending Figure* and Lisel Mueller's *Alive Together,* I select W. H. Auden's *Collected Works,* a volume of Gerard Manley Hopkins and one by Emily Dickinson.

Louise Gluck was my teacher at Goddard College's MFA program, and Lisel Mueller was my professor and internship supervisor at Elmhurst College in my undergrad days. I hope that in rereading their work I will relive those days when they and I believed that I would one day be a very good poet. I kept a poem written during my days at Goddard on which Louise Gluck had written about a particular line that described the roses in my grandmother's garden as "a deep ancestral red": "I wish I had written this." Now rereading their work I realize how seriously I have traitored my talent through disuse and misuse, how I have subverted their faith in me and sunk their investment in my success; how I have simply blown it by not realizing how privileged my time with them was. And how short youth and its sanctioned apprenticeships really are. Gerard Manley Hopkins I select because I remember his poem "Pied Beauty," and I want to soak myself in his sound, the luxurious pleasure of assonance and consonance, soft *O* on soft *O*, hard-boned *N*'s and *G*'s against *K*'s and *T*'s. I want my brain to step to the cadence of his lines. I find the poem quickly and read it slowly, twice.

The biographical material I read on him surprises me. Why did I never know he was a Jesuit priest? I knew he'd converted from the Anglican to the Roman Catholic Church, the reverse of my spiritual journey, but I didn't know his journey had led him to the priesthood. He was considered a mystic, and his poems weren't published until after his death. His story is more proof that the line between prayer and poetry is exceedingly thin. And that the appreciation of nature itself borders on prayer. There is a plaque in one of the other cells at Desert House that proclaims "For one who prays, all nature is Silent Praise."

My mother was right; I read too much. The reading keeps me from writing or thinking. It keeps me from talking and making a decent dinner, just as it kept me from playing or sports or piano when I was little. Here at Desert House I am returning to the habits of childhood and trying to break my old reading records. In summer, when I was little, I would read a book a day, seven books a week, not even stopping for Sunday. I have read more than two books a day since I've been here. But there are so many books and so little time.

Because I am reading voraciously and greedily, not chewing properly or tasting slowly like a gourmand, the flavors of the books run together and get mixed up in my head. It's like gobbling the green beans and mashed potatoes and pork roast in one big forkful. I wonder what happens when you mix Annie Dillard and John Climacus, Raymond Carver and Dom Hubert Zeller, Julian of Norwich and *Birds of North America*, Simon Tugwell and Lisel Mueller. It probably does justice to none of the authors, but it does make for an experience as unique as your own special blend of DNA. It's not pure, it's not single malt, but it is glorious.

I hear my mother's voice and wonder whether I'm hallucinating. "Get outside and get some fresh air and put that damn book down."

I look at my watch and discover I've been reading for five hours. I missed meditation and Vespers and am in serious danger of missing dinner. I drop my book and run out.

Dinner is again a sensual delight. A spicy chili and Spanish rice, freshly made tortilla chips and guacamole, flan, and guava and papaya. There are orgasmic noises coming forth from even the shyest and most proper of the guests. One of them mourns that Rina can't be with us on Sunday.

"Why not?" I ask. "Is she going away?" Lillian then explains that Sunday is the day that the staff and guests make the community dinner so Rina can make Sunday dinner for her own family.

"Who made the dinner last Sunday?" Lillian replies, "Nick and I. We like to do it."

All of this food makes me want to cook, too. I volunteer to help this Sunday. I want to make tomato cantaloupe soup, a cold soup I used to make for my gourmet cooking club. Maybe the aptitude and inclination tests I took during my career counseling sessions were right: I could be happy as a chef. But then again, happier yet as a musician, painter, or writer. Advertising was on the list, too, although finding out that you have an aptitude for a business that you are leaving because you're sick of it and it is sick of you is not the kind of thing that you want to hear or spread around.

I volunteer to wash the dishes tonight. It is so hot and dry that I think I'll enjoy immersing my hands in water for forty-five minutes or so. I can also stand and space out over the sink and not have to keep my wits about me in the heavy traffic of the tiny kitchen filled with people who don't know where anything goes and constantly change direction.

God always waits for me no matter how late I am.

After dinner I notice a commotion next to the Desert House office. Furniture is being carried out of one of the rooms; ladders, paint cans, and rollers go in, and there is lots of hammering and general hubbub. A teenage boy seems to be in charge.

"What's going on?" I ask him quietly. It's no intrusion on his personal silence since he's not a retreatant.

"We are making a place for Miss Trudy," he says with a strong Spanish accent. "I am in charge of the painting." Then he adds "But this is just my side job. I am an artist."

I ask him if he's a painter or a sculptor. He says he is a mask maker. He makes modern interpretations of traditional Mexican and Indian masks and is trying to get an exhibition in a Tucson gallery. He has all his masks on slides and carries them in his backpack. He wants to show them to me sometime when he stays for dinner.

I think how together he is for someone so young. Later I mention this to Nick. He laughs.

"How old do you think Tony is?"

"I don't know. Seventeen or eighteen."

"He's twenty-eight and has a daughter. That's why he works on houses, so he can bring home the bacon. You can't do that being a mask maker."

I'm still amazed. His commitment to his art is shaming to all of us who claim to be artists or writers with day jobs that take up too much time. He has a day job and a night job and a family and still manages to create.

It makes me wonder what I did with all my free time when I was younger. There was plenty of time to write but I didn't choose to. Couldn't I have skipped a mediocre movie, passed on yet another art crowd party, or backed out of a date I'd made with someone I didn't even want to be with?

I could have, but I didn't choose that. St. Augustine said, "It is our choosing that makes us what we are." I chose to be in advertising and chose not to be a poet, just as now I choose to be unemployed, a drifter looking not for work but for a calling.

I go back to the kitchen for ice water from the big water cooler. As I drink I notice a sign-up sheet on the bulletin board. Father Kane is asking for volunteers to keep the all-night vigil of the Blessed Sacrament. Many of the slots are already filled. I pencil my name in for midnight-to-one and hope I'll be able to stay awake since I'm having trouble making it past nine o'clock with the fresh air and early mornings here.

There are other postings on the boards. Notices about other retreats, including one that Sister Genny will be leading in a wooded area of Kansas. I didn't think there were any woods in Kansas, that it was just a big flat canvas for tornadoes to brush, but the pen-and-ink drawing of the setting makes it look very inviting.

There are also appreciative notes from repeat re-treatants, and near gushes from first-timers who felt the holiness of the place. It is a mark of the special-ness of Desert House that it has this following. I, too, feel it is holy and want to come back again. I want to share this experience with friends. Well, not too many friends, since part of its charm is that the community

is small and the promise of space inherent in the landscape isn't broken here as it is at other, bigger retreat
settings.

The seemingly innocent bulletin board has presented
yet another temptation. I am once again avoiding pen
and paper, the indescribable terror of the blank page.
I don't want to blow this opportunity as I've blown
so many others. I shuffle through the gravel back to
Thomas to face my demon or my muse.

Back at my desk in the hard-seated chair I show evidence of industry to my superego judge: ten years'
worth of weekly entries in the journals I keep for each of
my children; daily morning pages I did last fall for my
Artist's Way workshop; notes for poems and stories and
screenplays I keep in the projects section of my daily
agenda book. I present the countless television com-
mercial scripts for Lowenbrau and Michelob, Kibbles
'n Bits and Kraft Singles, and 7-Eleven, and The Big
Red Boat that now fill boxes in my basement and once
clogged the airwaves of America. I exhibit the funny but
instructive speeches I delivered to advertising wannabes
and brand managers and owners of major companies.
After viewing this output, though, Judge Superego remains unmoved. Like God, she knows I am just kidding
myself if I think any of this counts.

No muse meets me. It's Demon Day.

But what about raising three wonderful human beings who were once all in diapers at the same time? What about my world-class juggling of home and love and deaths and work? Judge Superego ignores these pleas, hands me a pen, and tells me to write. So I do.

Since I said I was writing prayers, friends have asked me for my definition of prayer. My answer has been that it's any conversation with God that acknowledges his power or moves one closer to her. Sometimes that makes for brittle standoffish prayers that hide behind a formal structure, and sometimes it makes for outpourings whose honesty frightens me.

In general, my prayers seem to divide into the angry and inquisitive on one hand and songs of praise on the other. They are the work of a soul divided, that soul perhaps being divided by God and therefore valuable in some way because of this very division.

Later I write about what I did on my walk today:

The Chosen

I have water to spare.
With whom shall I share?
Shall I choose
the brownest and smallest
or the greenest and tallest?

Shall I pick the weak
or the tough,
give it all to one
or give two barely enough?

I make a mockery
of natural selection,
pick the middlingest
for my affection:
the ordinary cholea,
the common echinacea.
The ones we gods all overlook
when the gifts are given
and the pleasure taken.

Today I set a thousand centuries right.
My grace rains down though the sun shines bright.
I hear them swallow loudly, unashamed.
I've engineered the triumph of the plain.

I sleep the sleep of the unjust. Fitful, dreamy. My
plant watering is more effective than my writing, ad-
monishes Judge Superego. This meager output is not
enough to offset my crimes of dispassion, the neglect
of a God-granted talent. There must be more.

Day Five / Wednesday

The Refusal of Joy

Reliably and roosterless I again awake at 5:20 a.m. and open my journal to record last night's strange dream, one that unfolds like a film and centers on a pair of lavender boots. The dream bears no relationship to my spiritual reading or to the events of the previous day. Perhaps if I were a more skilled interpreter relationships would suggest themselves, but I see none now. I really want to go to meditation this morning so as soon as I finish the entry I walk to the chapel.

I like the ritual of the service — the bowing, the bells, the walk around the periphery of the chapel. It feels ancient or at least timeless. So little and yet so much is required of the meditator. The selection of a mantra is important, and the discipline of concentration on the task is key.

I keep rethinking my mantra choice even as we enter our private inside worlds and leave the outer one behind. Why is my inside world more distracting than the outside one? When I am thinking about an idea or planning lists or daydreaming or even driving down the highway, I can easily shut out the scenery, other people's questions, radios, televisions, the diesel hum of my own car. I can edit out the ugliness, the imperfection.

But as soon as I step into my inner kingdom, the population of neglected tasks, ignored talents, injured loved ones, sins of omission, and words unspoken beg my attention more compellingly than the solid world outside, the saguaro and the mountains and the endless sky. Outside me is silence, inside cacophony. It takes me a full five minutes just to adjust the volume, turn everything down to an ignorable hum of white noise.

I have changed my mantra for today to "I'm capable of the task. I'm capable of the task. I'm capable of the task." Not very poetic.

After a few rounds of resistance I'm caught in the flow of belief. "I think I can, I think I can." I remember my favorite Golden Book. How close my mantra is to the Little Engine That Could's! The Little Engine's is better, but I force myself to hold to plan.

Soon the bells ring and it's time for our mediation walk. I try to be conscious of each step I take, of trying to make it the most beautiful step I can take so it will enhance both my experience and that of the group.

Because you can feel other people's rhythms, and their missteps. An imperfect step affects the feeling of the group, its aura. I feel caught up in the collective soul. There are no bad people here. I resist no one. I don't resist the groupness of it all.

After the bells ring us back into our meditations, I fall so deeply through the levels that I sleep.

The next set of bells reawakens me to the world. I put on my shoes and prepare for the sweet voicings of Morning Prayer. This being my fifth day, I am starting to feel confident in the routine of things, sure of where to sit and when to sing and how to hit the stresses of the psalms.

So now I stay in one of the two rows close to the altar, the place where the good singers sit.

I look forward to the songs and hope that Genny sits on my side of the altar. She has a beautiful, strong voice that balances and even overshadows the deepness of the men's voices, of Nick and Father John's confident volume. Genny's voice soars without lightening. It doesn't lose energy at the peaks.

I've fallen into the habit not only of calling rooms by their first times (as in Thomas or Bede or Henry) but also of dropping the honorific "Sister" in front of the nuns' names. Not because I am disrespectful, but because everyone here calls them by their first names.

Sister Philip is called Philip. Sister Rosina is called Rosina. I'm sure it makes them feel less apart, which is really the whole spirit of Desert House. These religious may not be of the world, but they are definitely in it. They look like you and me and dress only slightly more modestly.

Genny does sit on my side and I sing very loudly. I earn not only God's approval but a substantial breakfast of date nut bread, muesli, strawberries, cantaloupe, and two cups of coffee. Desert House is a temple of purification, but fortunately it's not an ascetic ashram despite the meditation.

My hiking, like my singing, is now confident. I am sure of my route, alert to the landmarks, discerning about what constitutes a path and what does not. Being unafraid of danger or disorientation frees me to think and write in my head. I tick off each trail marker on my mental list without missing a beat: the rusted-out Camaro; the well; the right and left forks on the Geddes ranch; the white metal gate to Saguaro National Forest; the black road to the abandoned mines; the cave in the westerly mountains. It makes me smile to think how skittish I was just five days ago. So self-congratulatory am I that I almost don't notice the diamondback rattlesnake. Just as I pass through the narrow, tree-covered trail leading into the wide wash it is resting in the sun on a flat, dusty rock. The snake's beige and white colors blend so perfectly with the rock's that I'm less than a foot from it when I finally make out its shape.

My heart is beating like a hummingbird's wings. So much for confidence. Today I carry a walking stick, but what would I have done with the stick if the diamondback had struck? Probably nothing. It would be hard to run away in the deep sand-like dust of the wash. The snake would have speed on its side. But this snake had already decided today was a perfect day for a nap and didn't lift head or tail when I came by. Maybe this snake was so used to hikers that it considered them barely worthy of notice. Boring, the way zoo animals eventually must regard the hordes of humans who come to see them every year.

Two-and-a-half hours later I'm back at Thomas. I take a long shower and put on the lightest weight cotton clothing I have. With all the changes of clothing my hikes require, I've already nearly filled my laundry bag. Guests are responsible for their own laundry so I'll need to make time for it soon. I've seen them hanging their sheets and clothing on the lines outside and am actually looking forward to it. I haven't hung wash out since I was a little girl and helped my grandmother put out the sheets in her backyard. I remember what fun it was to run through the wet sheets in summer. It might be even more fun here in the desert heat.

I return a stack of books to the library and get more. Evelyn Waugh's *Acedia/The Seven Deadly Sins, Praying with Catherine of Siena* by Patricia Mary Vinje, *The Hermitage Journals* by John Howard Griffin, *How to Meditate* by Sebastian Temple.

I lift the wooden side handle on my recliner to raise the footrest and read Waugh's thoughts on sloth. How appropriate that I am reading them in a La-Z-Boy. My attention is caught by a passage that looks at sloth in a way I've never thought of before: "The malice of Sloth lies not merely in the neglect of duty, but in the refusal of joy."

I do a personal inventory of my own instances of laziness. On the whole I've been very good at attending to duty, if you don't count the refusal to file my papers. There are times when I've been too lazy, though, to see someone else's need. It wasn't conscious, but in many ways I chose to minimize my interactions with people so they wouldn't demand of my time, my talent, my effort. If you see no pain but your own, there is little call to do anything for anyone.

I'd covered this territory many times before either in formal confession or private sackcloth sessions in the time before sleep. What was new was this refusal-of-joy aspect.

What joy had I denied both of us by not taking a leave of absence and caring for my sister Kim in the last months before her death from brain cancer? Could we have known each other more deeply, could I have developed qualities of soul or mind that would have made me happier today? Could I have eased her passage by my presence? The rational answer was that I had a newborn infant and couldn't care for anyone else, but sometimes joy requires an irrational look at the situation, a leap of faith and confidence into the unknown or the difficult.

What joy had I denied myself by not disciplining myself to write in my premarriage twenties and early thirties, by not making the effort to publish or use my connections to those who could help me?

What joy had I denied my family by not following my dream? Would I be a better mother and wife if I were happier in my work?

What joy had I denied my friend Colleen by refusing to see that she needed emotional support after the death of her parents? Would she be a happier person now, would I have been able to deal better with my sister's and father's deaths, or been better able to comfort my mother and my other sister, Leslie?

90

I would never know the answers to those questions now. All I could do was to understand the issues of sloth and joy I had yet to face and be better equipped to frame them when they arise.

I'm tired. This is demanding reading, even though I'm racing through Waugh's work. It's past twelve when I realize it's time for lunch. I need the break.

After lunch I intend to read more, but within moments I move from the recliner and lamp to the bed and then to the world of sleep. I don't wake up until four o'clock.

Now I want to stretch and hike, not an advisable activity in the peak heat of the afternoon, but a necessary one to get my blood moving. I decide to explore the back area of the complex that leads out to a small mountain. I'd found some hand-drawn maps in a portfolio in the dining room bookcases that showed the distance as about a quarter mile north of the Stations of the Cross.

The underbrush is a lot thicker than I thought, with no clear paths. Careful as I am about avoiding cactus spines, I get two caught in my bare calf and have to pull them out. I should have worn long pants. I hadn't thought at all about how dense pathless desert would be. I make it out to within several feet of the mountain, but it no longer seems interesting enough to risk more brushes with cacti. I remember the cautionary tale my Arizona Stagecoach driver told me about the jumping cactus and don't want to risk being jumped by an airborne cactus ear. They don't really jump you, but when they dry out and the wind blows hard it can send them flying with a force that seems volitional, even malevolent.

I can't wait for a change of clothes and an unventuresome Vespers in the chapel.

At dinner I confess to Lillian that I'd taken an unintentional nap this afternoon and felt unbearably unproductive and unspiritual.

She laughs. "Now you know why we call this place 'The Desert House of Naps.'"

"You mean it happens to everyone?"

"All the time. It's part of the seductive allure of the place."

Other guests who hear our interchange offer their own confessions of secret naps as though they were confessing having masturbated in their cloistered cells. Their stories don't make me feel better.

"But I'm not here to sleep" I say indignantly. "I'm here to write and think and read and center myself for a new phase of my life." What a prig. Had I really said that?

Before I can succumb to the perverse delight of self-flagellation, a lovely, lilting Irish voice joins in. I turn to see it's that of Sister Patsy, who came to Desert House after spending two years as a missionary in Africa.

"Don't be so serious, love." She laughs. "God works in mysterious ways. You see, sleep is a form of grace. God sent you sleep because you need rest from the travails of this world. There's nothing like a good nap to center your soul, anyway, or a good dream, if you can remember it. It's a gift."

"Do you nap?" I ask bluntly.

"As much as God lets me get away with" she twinkles.

I like Patsy very much. Her lightness of being is refreshing. As refreshing as a good nap.

Nick and Patsy ask me if I've seen much outside the compound.

I say I've pretty much stuck to campus and am afraid I'll get distracted from my purpose if I go to town.

"But you can't leave without seeing the film of the desert at the museum" says Nick. "It will make you appreciate your surroundings even more."

"Well, I did want to learn more about desert life...."

"We have a date then. I'm taking Patsy up to the museum next week and you can come with us."

After dinner I write letters to each of my children and to my husband. I'm careful to talk about a different aspect of life here in each, so they can exchange letters or offer little nuggets of news that the others don't know. Then, since I'm in the groove, I write my mother, probably the first letter I've written to her in my life since I always went home for all the big holidays and never stayed away long enough to send more than a postcard. It feels good to send outward messages after living so much inside myself these past few days.

Writing letters is a good exercise. It makes me want to write more, so I do instead of taking refuge in one of my books. Ten o'clock. It's time to sleep now. Before I turn off the light I notice the gray splotchy corpses of the tiny bugs I've martyred, marring the otherwise pure white walls. I ask God to forgive me my murderous deeds. I also make a mental note to wash the walls tomorrow. And then I write a prayer to atone for the joy I've snuffed out in so many small ways.

The Murderer's Prayer

God, stop me before I kill again.
Before I kill the mood or
quell the laughter.
Before I snuff out my talent
or just kill time.
Before I criticize and deride,
derail a project or a plan,
squelch a spirit or decimate a man.
Inspire me to listen closely,
to add to an idea rather than subtract,
to be not a sitter on the sidelines
but one who acts.
Let me be the one who saves the day,
revives the spirit,
gives each dream its due.
Help me grow to be more like You.

The Face in the Tree

I wake up feeling that I am God's creature, a wild animal like Prairie, my children's pet prairie dog.

I imagine God watches me the way we watch Prairie: observes me, enjoys me, can't wait to see what I will do next in my charming innocence. God notes what frightens me, what makes me happy, what I prefer to eat, how I differ from other creatures. God sends the wind to pet me.

I want to be God's pet, albeit uncaged. I like imagining God's joy in the simple fact that I am, that I belong to her. I wish I could keep this feeling.

I love wild animals. At dinner last night I heard Trudy talking about the mother fox and her baby who have been coming to feed at her hermitage, the one called Bede. I invited myself to come and await their arrival tonight, which she says usually happens around 8:30 or so, just as the sun sets. I have never seen a fox up close. Trudy says she sets out sliced apples and fresh water to attract them. The baby always comes first. The mother waits behind a bush to make sure nothing attacks the baby.

I want to see a javalina, too. Nick says they are boars, travel in hunting packs, and smell really foul. You can usually smell them before you see them. They release this odor from their musk glands because they are near-sighted and smell is how they find each other and stick together in a herd. A javalina eats the roots of cacti, and some can weigh as much as fifty-five pounds.

I'm also curious to see what the inside of one of the hermitages is like. It sounds really scary to live by one's self, separate enough from the dorm-like setting of the rest of the campus that you can't see the buildings and no one in the buildings can see you. During the day the quarter-mile distance isn't very daunting, but in darkness the little hermitage might as well be in space. Could anyone hear you scream? But this very isolation is also what makes Bede so alluring. Away from noise and lights and footsteps, amazing encounters with the desert wildlife would be possible, as well as deeper immersion in one's inner life. On the other hand, there are no locks on the doors. I am trying to work up the courage to request a room change to a hermitage for my second week's stay.

Meditation and Morning Prayer don't feel compelling, but I drag myself to chapel anyway. I need discipline in my daily routine, a regular time to feed my soul, to read, to write, to exercise in the same way a baby needs regularity in its feeding and sleeping schedule to thrive and to grow. It's a way to create a rhythm. In my old life in the advertising business, I had a schedule of meetings that filled every waking moment, but I let others determine how I'd spend my days and allowed any crisis to blow up a carefully crafted morning or steal my time to think and create. Poor self-management. I have to start now to create a horarium designed to honor my personal values.

After a healthy breakfast I am ready to hike again. I've taken to wearing my blue crystal rosary around my neck as a talisman to ward off evil. It's sort of like the garlic-versus-vampires theory. The prospect of accidentally confronting snakes and bobcats doesn't scare me nearly as much as the idea of encountering a creep lurking in the mountains or malingering on a narrow trail, and I am certain even the most evil of men would hesitate before harming a woman wearing a rosary.

The trails and landmarks have now become so familiar that I don't really see them anymore. I'm inside myself, seeing pictures from experiences I'm yet to have.

Sister Jeanne has promised to take me to an ancient tree with a detailed face carved into its trunk. It is reputed to have been created by a nomadic band of Hohokam Indians several hundred years ago. We're going to the tree right after dinner this evening and I'm imagining whether the face will be comforting or scary, a blessing or a warning.

Tomorrow morning Kate will guide me on a new hiking path. We hope to end up at the solstice at Picture Rocks by 11:30 a.m. The summer solstice doesn't technically take place until Saturday, June 21, but after eight hundred years and a lot of settling of the land beneath the cliff-like rocks, we're not sure it's still completely accurate so we're going to visit the site on both Friday and Saturday. Kate described how the light would trace the circle, but I'm skeptical that this will really happen.

After library and lunch I do laundry, reading in the dining room rocker between loads. Today I'm tackling *An Anthology of the Love of God* by Evelyn Underhill. She sees God even in the mundane and inglorious moments of life: "The dripping tap or barking dog which teaches patience is as much an instrument of God as the shattering blow which tears two souls apart."

Underhill forces me to reassess the interruptions I used to face every hour of my life. The constantly ringing phone, the shrill cries for Mommy to intervene in yet another sibling squabble, the cancelled family vacations due to yet another client crisis — maybe they are the stuff of spiritual redemption rather than rude interruptions in my quest for a state of grace.

Perhaps my definition of a state of grace needs revision. I have felt states of grace during two long periods of my life. The first lasted January 1986 through Easter of 1988 and the second ran from Christmas of 1992 through May 1994. During both these periods I felt in harmony with God. During both these periods there were not only happy instances of great good fortune but also many occasions for deepest sadness.

In the first state of grace I resumed writing after a long silence. I became a born-again virgin (by virtue of a self-imposed program of total abstinence), fell in love with the man who is now my husband and got married, spent three weeks in China, gave birth to my first child and bought a house. I also watched my sister die of a brain tumor and eulogized and buried my father. Three days a week for a year I made grueling flights to and from Battle Creek, Michigan, for business while nursing an infant and enduring the hostile takeover of my ad agency by a British holding company. It was the proverbial best of times and worst of times, but during all of it I never lost my center or the sense of God's presence in my life.

During the second state of grace there were no significant events. But I was surrounded by people I loved working with because of their immense talent and goodness, and I was overwhelmed by the joy of raising my three children and seeing them develop into interesting, likeable people of great sensitivity and humor. I was always conscious of how many blessings had been bestowed upon me. Minor irritations like never sleeping more than five or six hours a night and scarfing dinner out of the refrigerator didn't phase me.

Grace seems independent of events. It affects your perception of them and your opinion of your own ability to handle what comes your way.

I race through more Underhill: "Many people suggest by their behaviour that God is of far less importance than their bath or morning paper or early cup of tea."

If she were writing now instead of in 1953, she would doubtless cite television, the Internet, and going to the health club as the false gods we put before us. One of my neighbors said to me that she goes to her health club as though she was going to temple. Our bodies being temples of the Holy Ghost notwithstanding, it is a sad commentary on how much more we value the body than the soul.

I think about the hour I devoted to the TV show *Homicide* on too many Friday evenings, my numbed thumbings through *Vogue* and *Marie-Claire* while aloft. Time I could have spent reading or praying or meditating my way to a graceful center.

I skim further for nuggets that speak to me, probably not at a pace she intended the reader keep. I'm doing sixty in a twenty-mile-an-hour zone: "We need such silence and leisure as we get in Retreat; what one of the mystics called a rest most busy. 'Then the repressed elements of our truest being can emerge and get light and air.'"

I love this phrase "a rest most busy." It perfectly describes how I'm spending my days. In doing what the western world regards as "nothing" I am more mentally occupied and awake than I had been during the busiest eighteen-hour day in my former life. Nothing here demands that I go through the motions; it is all uncharted. My clock and my compass are inside me. When I am not required to do anything, there is more and more I choose to do.

I finish my book and check my laundry. In the desert sun my things are already dry, so dry they're nearly stiff. No wet sheets to run through. I hide from the sun in my room and decide to tackle another take on the spiritual life — Macrina Wiederkehr's *A Tree Full of Angels.* Father Kane had quoted her in one of his sermons. Wiederkehr had been to Desert House and may have written portions of the book here. Inside the cover is an inscription in the writer's hand: "May your seeking lead you into the eye of God."

Although my speed reading doesn't do her work justice, today hers is not the food I hunger for. Right now I want less poetry and more information from my reading. I flip past lovely turns of phrase housing true insights, such as "When I want to see clearly, I close my eyes" and "Sometimes we run away from home without leaving." At some other time they will feed me well. But today, I need harder truths. I need the confrontation I usually seek to avoid.

Grace seems independent of events. It affects your perception of them and your opinion of your own ability to handle what comes your way.

I put Wiederkehr down and pick up a pen, but nothing comes out. Maybe nothing is supposed to come out. Maybe the divine voice wants me to shut up and let it in. Maybe silence is the ultimate confrontation.

After dinner Sister Jeanne leads me down the unmarked trail to the face in the tree. It's very narrow and winds down a hillside to a dry gulch that's now used as a horse trail by drovers. The tree is an old but ordinary desert willow typically found in washes. It's not identified by any sort of marker and hasn't any sort of majestic or important approach. There are just a lot of dead branches on the ground and scattered piles of rock.

Yet the carved face is magical. It's not primitive and masklike, but very detailed and real looking, as though a talented sculptor took his or her time to make it as lifelike as possible. The wood of the tree where carved emerges as a warm, reddish brown. No one knows who carved the face but it is thought to have been a Native American whose tribe was passing through more several hundred years ago.

I stare into the eyes of the face that seem to look back at me, to follow me if I move to another vantage point. Jeanne and I carefully touch the cheeks to feel their smoothness.

The tree feels holy. We are slow and reverential in our movements. This face is an altar as fine as any cast from marble. After five more minutes of contemplation Sister Jeanne and I walk back to Desert House in silence.

Tonight is the night we will all sneak down to Bede to see the two foxes feeding. As darkness falls, we grab our flashlights and walk the quarter mile down to the hermitage. We watch for snakes and seem to see them everywhere they don't exist. "We" is me, Patsy, and

Philip (Sister Philip). We get sillier by the minute, the way thirteen-year-old girls get when they hear noises outside during sleepovers. We're walking on the road through Hell, even if it only leads to an innocuous little green house facing a tiny garden and watering hole.

When I slide open the screen and glass doors, we're greeted by an oven's blast of hot air. Patsy quickly turns on the evaporative cooling system, but the sound ruins the atmosphere and would drown out the rustling of any approaching foxes. We agree to run the system full blast until it gets semi-bearable and then shut it down so we can wait and watch and listen.

Trudy's recommended fox lure is cut-up Granny Smith apples. We busy ourselves slicing them, empty the clay watering dish and pour in fresh water from a pitcher. The cooling system is shut down, and the house is silent as we take up our sentry posts. I lie flat on the floor by the screen door.

Noises. We quietly admonish the quartet that enters: Nick, Kate, Lillian, and Trudy.

After fifteen minutes we lose faith. The foxes won't come. There are too many of us, or maybe they don't really like apples after all.

Then suddenly, soundlessly, the baby is at the clay dish drinking. The kit is unself-conscious, unaware of any danger or humans lurking just a few feet away. It drinks loudly. The mother creeps up behind a bush and watches. She seems nervous and paces the area near the watering hole and apple before coming up to take a bite. She takes one piece and retreats back to the bush. When the kit came up, it stayed while it ate, ready to take another piece. But then it had its mother to be wary for it.

In a few moments it's all over. Mother and son disappear, and we don't even see where or how. It's like a David Copperfield illusion. Did we really see the foxes or not?

We all head to our respective homes. On the way back I quietly ask Trudy if I can move into Bede, since she has moved most of her things to her new quarters near the office and it is available now. She seems pleased and says I may switch rooms on Monday if I would like. I'm scared but entranced by the prospect of living in my own little house even farther from human contact and closer to the animals than the rest of the cells and hermitages. I ask Trudy about my hermitage's namesake, and she tells me that it is named for Bede Griffiths, an English Benedictine who ran ashrams in India and later in California's Big Sur. His life's work was the union of Western contemplative prayer and Eastern meditation. That seems to be Father John Kane's purpose, too, since zen and the leanings of the Eastern mystics

are so gracefully intertwined with the Roman Catholic
services at Desert House.

I fall asleep imagining the daily life I will lead once I
move into Bede. Before I fall completely asleep, I jot a
prayer in my journal that reflects my musings on grace
earlier in the day. It is a kind of riff on Psalm 22.

Prayer in the Dark

> I believe you will come again.
> Maybe even tomorrow.
> Like the sun
> you have set on my soul
> many times,
> only to shine your face
> that much brighter
> upon your return.
> If you didn't go away
> how would I ever know
> you were here?

The Bad Seed

Up at 5:20 again, without alarm clock. Bells in my head have been rung by God. I have always been a morning person, but here my risings have migrated easterly, counterclockwise.

Morning pages are intended to be written stream of conscious and unexpurgated, before your first cup of coffee, before your first word to another human being. My morning pages here at Desert House have been surprising. Unlike the ramblings I jotted for nearly six months at 6:00 a.m. back home, these morning pages come out making sense, even if they are strange. They come out as stories, poems, and musings, instead of endless self-queries and complaints. It's as though my dreams are preparing me to be someone else.

This morning, however, my pages unnerve me. What streams from my pen is an imaginary account of my father's murder by me and my eventual ostracism from the family because of it.

I put down my pen. This is a hateful piece written in a voice not my own. It almost makes me believe in channeling. I tear it up and wash my hands. Out, out damned spot.

My father died of a heart attack at the age of sixty-two while driving home from a hockey game he'd played in. He died two months before my sister Kim died of a brain tumor and was therefore spared the intolerable pain of seeing his child die before him. My mother said my father had said he was trying to make a deal with God. He wanted to be taken so Kim could be spared. He also just wanted to die. I wrote his eulogy the night of his death and was surprised at the enormity of the loss I felt, and how much love lay beneath the veneer of resentment. I would never have murdered my father. It would be like murdering myself.

Retreat has a way of bringing everything out into the open, all the feelings that lie just below the surface and sometimes even deeper ones. The time in solitude is a purgative. All of my bad qualities and many of the good ones come up and demand to be seen. I see that my supposed hatred of my father is really hatred of myself, of the part of me that is most like him. I try to reassure myself that these dark thoughts are positive, remembering the words of Molly Ramanujan, my writing teacher at the University of Chicago: "Everything that is bad in life is good on the page." It is important to acknowledge and maybe even embrace all the darkness and light in my life, not only for the sake of a story, but for my own sanity. Passing judgment on my father makes me feel uncomfortable. I remember the origin of the word "devil," *diabolus,* which means tearing apart or division. When I separate my father from myself I leave myself divided and unwhole. I think about Satan, *satanus,* which means accusation. When I accuse my father, I accuse myself. When I accuse myself, I accuse God.

God is about wholeness, not separation. Since she gave birth to all, she can't reject any part nor bear our rejection of her creation. I compose a prayer.

Chosen

> Does God prefer the day or night,
> the clear or cloudy, the dark or light?
> The hot or cold, the slow or fast,
> dreams or waking, the present or past?
> How does God choose — start with ten best?
> Winnow and pare as they're put to the test?

I think God sees the good in all,
the warmth in winter, the spring in fall,
the life in death, the good in sin,
the love in hate, the her in him.
God cannot pick just half a soul
since God's the one who made the whole.

Then I get ready for the Friday celebration of the Eucharist at seven and for more elevating thoughts.

Friday is Hermit Day at Desert House. The only scheduled religious service is the Eucharist. The Office and meditation are left to the discretion of the retreatant. This is to be a day of total silence. No talking even at dinner. And like breakfast and lunch, will be eaten on one's own. The silence will not be broken until Saturday's evening meal.

I hike to the face in the tree after breakfast to meditate, and then take the path up and around the windmill. I have never encountered anyone on my previous hikes, but today on the way up the wash a woman on horseback approaches and asks directions to Picture Rocks. She tells me to speak slowly because she is deaf. I think about our different views of silence.

My hike is well-timed. At eleven thirty I arrive at the Picture Rocks sun clock to await the miracle of light. Kate is already there. We wait until noon but nothing happens. We haven't given the Hohokam tribe enough credit for their precision. The clock will come alive with light tomorrow on the real date of the summer solstice just as intended when it was painted several hundred years ago.

Back on the mail table in the dining room is a Federal Express package for me. I used to dread such packages at home because they would include videotapes of rough-cuts for commercials inside, roughcuts I would need to study for an hour. Then there would be the calls to the creative director, the creative team, and the pro-ducer. Then there would be the audiotrack of my own second-guessing playing through my head as I debated possible edits, better music, different line readings, and so on. I got many FedEx packages on every family va-cation, which meant I'd be on the phone or in front of a screen in a hotel room instead of in a pool swimming with my kids and playing.

This FedEx package is a happy one. Jim has sent me letters from himself and each of our children. I sit in the window rocker and read each one several times, happy for the connection.

After lunch, it is back to Thomas for reading and writing.

I settle in the La-Z-Boy and open Sebastian Temple's *How to Meditate* to see what tricks I can learn. There is a special section with recommendations on meditation for Westerners. I take notes on shadow gazing, a very ancient form of meditation that requires you to stand in sunlight so you can see your own shadow, then transfer your gaze to the blue sky and concentrate on the silvery afterimage of your shadow.

Having gleaned what I could from Temple, I turn next to *Praying with Catherine of Siena* by Patricia Mary Vinje. On page thirty I find a beautiful opening prayer written by St. Catherine: "May I come before the truth and have the courage to be honest in facing myself and the situations of life. May I come before the face of God and bring all that is hidden into the light."

I embrace this as my new Morning Prayer for its simplicity and brevity. It addresses two of my greatest sins: the fear of honesty and a tendency to hide what is unpleasant. I don't want to face what is difficult. I am afraid of facing God. Yet that is exactly what I will have to do tomorrow from midnight until one during my Blessed Sacrament vigil. I will be alone with my God in a side chapel lit only by candles. Alone with the Creator of heaven and earth, and of me.

I have chosen a spooky time to sit vigil, and a spooky place. The desert is where Christ met temptation, as did Moses and John the Baptist and prophets from nearly every faith. Midnight in the desert of good and evil.

And I will be there at the confrontation. I've always been afraid of being confronted by evil because I see myself as intrinsically flawed. Of course I am. That's what the Roman Catholic doctrine of original sin is all about. But when I was a child and I acted up or out my mother sometimes called me "the bad seed." She had a dark sense of humor and said it half-jokingly but it stung and it stuck nonetheless.

> *Retreat has a way of bringing everything out into the open, all the feelings that lie just below the surface and sometimes even deeper ones.*

I'd forgotten she called me that, but when I was thirty-two I had a nightmare that I was eight years old and being interrogated by a Southern sheriff about the murder of a classmate at a school picnic. The dream alarmed me so much that I asked my mother if anyone in my class had ever died mysteriously. She could think of no one.

Then one night my sister Kim called me and said, "Remember that dream you had about murdering someone as a child?"

"Yes," I said fearfully. "Do you remember who it was?"

"No," she laughed. "I just watched it on TV. It's the plot of a movie called *The Bad Seed* and it was made in the fifties. Don't you remember? That's why Mom called you that when we were kids. You must have seen it with her and forgotten."

I was so relieved to find out that the murder was just a result of a bad soup of memories I'd whipped up in my head.

I felt cleansed. I forgave myself for yet another murder, that of the child within me. I have been an adult for so very long.

In the late afternoon, I fill an empty votive holder with water and put it outside my screen door to attract small birds, a doll's house birdbath. The water looks like melted candle wax, and the sun glowing in the sky sets the surface aflame. The candle has no wick, yet it burns.

I hadn't been smart enough to think of the small birdbath on my own. A curve-billed thrasher peered through the screen door and yelled at me, and I interpreted this as asking for a drink mainly because when I looked out I could see that the clay watering dish was dry. I could simply have refilled the dish, but then the thrashers would have left my doorway.

My beggar bird and another come to the bird glass. They politely drink a sip and then talk to each other earnestly and quietly. I wonder whether they are deciding whether to trust me. The birds walk away. I feel rejected. I think they think I'm making fun of them, trying to make them look like those silly mechanical drinking birds. Or maybe they don't like my choice of glassware. The votive does have a jelly jar look; they must sense it's not the kind of glass you'd serve to honored guests. Also, it must be really odd and unnatural to be able to see your water from the side like this. I can't think of a good example in nature, no streams or rivers with transparent banks. A waterfall is open on all sides, but these birds have clearly never seen a waterfall.

There's just enough time after Vespers and dinner for some reading and writing.

This evening I open *The Hermitage Journals* by John Howard Griffin. It is a perfect way to christen my own hermitage stay. Griffin quotes from Cassian: "We pray best when we no longer know we are praying."

While it questions the worthiness of my attempts to structure new prayers, I understand what Cassian means. There have been times when I have lost sight of the boundaries between me and God. Curiously, they were not when I was high on grace, but when I was brought low by a series of failures in the sight of the world. I lost all pretense, all desire to create prettiness in my prayer, and just spoke to God in an unedited rush. I did not resist God seeing me as I was.

This should not have been the occasion for me to write a prayer, but I did.

Gradual

> I want to know you, Lord.
> But I must approach you slowly
> for fear of losing myself in you.
> Every move you make toward me
> seems aggressive.
> Every move I make toward you
> feels weak, submissive.
> But still I go forward, knowing that
> refusing you would be a bigger loss
> than that of my self.

I wanted to smoke a cigarette, though if I had one I'd choke on it. I wanted to go outside and see the stars.

I sat out in my chair and watched for stars and the starlike headlights of distant cars on the invisible highway. I held a vigil for all the comforting lights God gives us to make it through the night.

Tomorrow the former bad seed would sit vigil for the Blessed Sacrament.

Day Eight / Saturday

Vigilante

Today I would keep two vigils: the first at Picture Rocks, waiting for the solstice to mark the first day of summer, and the second at the Chapel of our Lady of Solitude, acknowledging the Blessed Sacrament as deity.

I set out on a silent hike before Kate's and my appointed meeting time of eleven thirty. After a mile of hiking, my mind, like the landscape and the wind, is still.

How can I communicate the magic of living in silence? Every word I type violates its spirit, as ink violates the purity of a white page. Silence gives you primary experience undiluted by another's interpretation. Silence gives you the unexpurgated version of yourself. It delivers you of the obligation to respond to other people's words. It doesn't bend you in the direction of another's choosing. In silence it's just you and God.

Silence is a void of sorts, a vacuum. Since nature abhors a vacuum, what rushes in to fill the silence? Unwanted thoughts, shelved insights: the censored and the impolite fight to occupy the space that silence opens up.

It is dangerous to live in silence. You're more vulnerable to attack by what you fear most. In the desert's loneliness there is no mother to pat your head and tell you you're a good boy or girl. There are no visible enemies on whom to safely unleash your anger. There are no dogs to kick or others to blame. No familiar routine to cling to.

Silence is a reverse universe. It's like having a sound camera that only records the negative of what we hear. It captures unspoken sounds our brains then choose to develop into what we can acceptably hear. Do we have any thoughts that are not formed by others? Could we have any thoughts without others to inform them, shape them, hear them? Our very language is the choice of those who came before and deemed particular objects and actions namable and notable. Our constructs are not our own except in that we don't reject the constructs with which we're presented.

So maybe silence lets us hear the voices of others. The words we've ignored, the epithets we've secretly taken to heart, the eponyms we've tried for so long to outrun — black sheep, daddy longlegs, lazy, skinny, serious, the not-so-pretty-one, everybody's second choice. It lets us hear advice untaken, instincts ignored, the small voice unheeded. When the voices subside, then there is a long, long pause. A pause even longer than the kind we tritely label as pregnant. If you wait long enough the first words you hear sound like the truth you've been hoping you'd stumble upon.

At 11:25 I arrive at the Rocks. Kate isn't there yet, so I sit down and study the petroglyphs, pale yellow-white markings pecked into the weathered gray rock. There is a spiral sun, people, coyotes, and horned sheep set to honor the agrarian Hohokam tribe who lived here for a time.

Since our last visit to the Rocks I've done some reading about the Hohokam. It seems they were at this site several hundred years ago (apparently no one's been able to do conclusive dating so this figure is merely an educated guess) and regarded it as one of the most exceptionally beautiful spots in the Tucson Mountains. Because of its beauty they called it sacred and left the legacy of the glyphs. The head-dressed dancing human figures give the glyphs their distinctively Hohokam cast. Shamans or hunters, the ones who usually functioned as symbol makers, would have been the ones responsible for pecking out the deer, antelope, and mountain sheep shapes on the Rocks to ensure a successful hunt.

One interpretation given for the peckings is that when food was needed, a sacred ritual was performed. Pictures of animals would be pecked into the rocks, and prayerful pardon would be asked of the animals being hunted.

The rocks are volcanic so my guessing that the black sand-like granules might be lava remnants isn't as off the mark as Kate made me think. There may be black sand lava and coal traces coexisting here.

At precisely 11:30 Kate and the first dot of light at the center point arrive. In excited but respectful silence we watch the dot of light expand into a triangle that grows ever larger between where nine and twelve would be on the clockface were the face enumerated. At exactly noon the dot on twelve lights up so brightly it looks phosphorescent. Perfect time, after hundreds of years! I feel connected to everyone who has come before me. I wonder if the Hohokam artists imagined how powerfully future audiences would react to their work.

Kate and I quietly separate, and I take a long nap before meditation, sleeping off the intoxication of witnessing something so ancient prove its relevance in the modern world.

After dinner I'm so restless I can't read.

I'd had a cup of coffee because I wanted to be alert for the vigil, but the jolt of caffeine rendered me useless for any sort of reflection or quietude. I have to keep moving.

I borrow a flashlight and go for a night walk around the grounds. It's easier to hear the desert wildlife than to see it, although I think I catch an occasional flash of a chuckwalla, zebra-tailed lizard, or Harris antelope squirrel scurrying through the brittlebush and burro-bush. I head for my regular daytime trail but after a few hundred yards decide it's a foolish chance to take for someone who had trouble telling trails from mean-ingless spaces between creosote bushes. I have to own up to my limitations. Since I can't tell a bullnose from a diamondback, I don't want to have any more meet-ings with remarkable snakes. I've since read that there are coral snakes out here, too. While I'd memorized the classic Old West saying to help me identify the dangerous ones — "red and yellow kill a fellow, red and black, friend of Jack" — I wasn't sure the words would come out in the right order in a face-to-fang encounter.

I walk back up to Bede to see if the foxes will come. I wait for awhile in a chair out front but decide they won't come without apple bait.

I go back up to the compound kitchen for ice water and crackers. Holly, the Desert House dog, is cooling herself off outside the sliding door. I pet her and she closes her eyes. I feel sorry for Holly. She wants to belong to someone so much, some one person, but she has to stay a community dog because she's not allowed inside and retreatants are discouraged from inviting Holly into their rooms. Guests used to take Holly on hikes with them into the Saguaro National Forest, but the Park Rangers cracked down and would send the hiker and Holly back to Desert House so she pretty much got confined to the grounds. I think she needs a kid to play with. Someone silly and unsilent.

When I walk past the office I notice a sign I hadn't seen before, affixed to the window like one of those Pinkerton's security stickers. "Protected by Angels" it says. I believe it is.

At midnight I enter the main chapel doors. It's dark and quiet. To my right the door is cracked open slightly so soft light lines the jamb. A pair of shoes sits outside the door next to a small mat. I'm not sure of the etiquette or protocol, whether I should wait for the present vigilant to exit, or whether I should quietly enter to let her know that her time is up.

I slip off my shoes, enter, and bow toward the host in the ciborium on top of the altar. The ciborium displays a consecrated host held within a glass circle and surrounded by golden sun rays. Consolata, an older nun whose aura clashes badly with my own, is the vigilant.

I immediately feel I've violated her space and done the wrong thing, that I should have waited outside.

But there is no going back so I move behind and far back from her, sit down, and bless myself. I look around at the small stained-glass windows and at the red and white candles of all sizes burning near the altar. There is a small soft pillow that acts as a kneeler directly in front of the ciborium.

Consolata sighs heavily and then leaves without acknowledging my presence. I am relieved to hear the chapel doors close behind her. I want to touch the host in the ciborium but am afraid something awful will happen to me if I do. Maybe the ground would swallow me. The wind picks up and whistles threateningly through the slightly open windows. The candles flicker. I wonder whether they could all go out at once, or whether an evil presence could cause them to create darkness right in God's own house.

I move to the pillow so I can be closer to God and safer from evil.

After praying for some time and staring at the host, I feel God's love for me and get brave. I rise from my knees, go up to the ciborium, and pet the host.

Nothing happens. I'm not struck down and don't feel sacrilegious or blasphemous. I feel happy and holy.

Maybe even God gets tired of reverential distance and wants intimacy, too, just like the most reticent of us.

Soon Genny enters the room. She blesses herself and sits in the back until I rise to leave. Then she moves forward to the pillow, just as I had done earlier. Some rituals are instinctive.

I'm glad I signed up to be a vigilant. God's vigilante. The former bad seed.

Back at Thomas I write a bedtime prayer:

Vigil

All I do is wait.
I wait for your call.
I wait for your voice.
I wait for ecstasy
only to find
you've been here with me
all along.
Then I wait and I wait and I wait
for your rebuke,
which never comes.

Day Nine / Sunday

Scorpion

After seven days at Desert House I'm completely with the program. It's not a deprivation or a difficulty for me not to speak; I prefer it. Years of being in a business that was all talk and team, meetings and diplomacy have made me happy to give my tongue and ears a rest.

Years of synthesizing the thoughts of others and compromising to reach agreement have left me wondering what my own private undiluted opinions might actually be. With so much overcommunication, does anyone truly know the integrity of her own mind? Desert House is a good way to dechaff your ideas. There is no boss or client to act as unwitting screen.

This is what I think about walking to chapel for Eucharist. Today, like every day, is bright and sunny. It is impossible to suffer seasonal affective disorder in the Sonoran Desert, impossible not to feel the hope of the Eucharist as the host rises in unison with the sun. Its rays render every face holy and irradiates Father John Kane's vestments so that he seems a prophet directly sent to speak to our small community. It lends credence to his assertion that everything at Desert House revolves around the Resurrection.

There is a strong sense of community here, even with a population whose mix changes every few days as new retreatants enter and old ones return to the world. This is real community, not a manufactured one. There are no prescribed or enforced rules of behavior besides the respect for another's mental space. There is no jockeying for position, no reward to be gained for being perceived as a better retreatant or a more helpful person or a leader. It would be futile and counterproductive to try to assert dominance here or even to be the life of the party. I am excited because today being Sunday, Rina's day off, Nick and Lillian and I will prepare the food for the talking dinner. Nick is making lasagna, Lillian is making a coconut cake, and I will make my tomato cantaloupe soup. My husband sent me the recipe from *The Vegetarian Gourmet* cookbook I haven't opened in eleven years.

My Sunday hike is down the road in the direction of the town of Cortaro. I make it almost to town, right to the railroad tracks where I saw the dust devils a week ago, and then decide it isn't worth going further.

I am bored following the highway and miss the fillip provided by hiking where there is no road, where you might accidentally veer off the trail and go somewhere you weren't supposed to be.

As Desert House comes in sight I have a strong sense of coming home and settle in for a read in the corner chair in Thomas.

I'd decided to do some reading about Desert House itself. I didn't really want to know too much about it before I came, preferring to meet it as a stranger and without any preconceptions that reality might prove disappointing. But now that I am here and have absorbed it on my own terms, I am curious about its birth and lineage and about the people who infused it with its wonderful spirit.

Its seed of inspiration came from a Redemptorist named Father Bernard Häring. His name graces the entrance to the common room where we take our dinners, and there is a bust of him in the chapel. Father Bernard felt that God was calling him to a life of prayer and requested permission to join the monastic Trappists. His superiors challenged him instead to lead a life of prayer within the Redemptorist Order. He accepted their challenge and founded several houses of prayer with the guidance of Thomas Merton.

Later Father John Kane, also a Redemptorist, felt moved to found a house of prayer in the desert. He learned all he could from Bernard Häring's experience, and in 1974 he began building Desert House of Prayer on thirty-one acres of primitive high desert land densely covered by cacti, brush, and desert trees. Father Kane named the chapel Our Lady of Solitude because he said that Mary could not have become the Seat of Wisdom or the Hearer of the Word without having sounded the height and depth of solitude.

Over the years Desert House guests have included a very diverse group: Protestants; Orthodox Catholics who appreciate that *Jesus Prayer,* an Eastern rite tradition, has found a home in contemplative prayer here; Jews; Hindus; Buddhists; and Native Americans. Some of the Native Americans who visit say that ten-thousand-foot Safford Peak, within direct site of Desert House, is a holy mountain. Even those who belong to no declared religion visit and are moved to pray by the intense spiritual vibrations of the land and the community. A number of writers and artists come here for the energy to begin or complete their projects.

I, too, feel what they do and understand why Desert House remains a mecca for those who seek to renew their faith or tap into their creativity. This is indeed a place of prayer. It is also the right moment to write a prayer of my own.

Prayer for a New Voice

Give rest to my internal voice, dear God,
a voice I often confuse with yours.
But your voice doesn't
suck the air out of the room
or the thoughts out of my head.
Your words are light and spare;
I breathe them like air.
Speak not to me
but for me.
Let me fall silent
and hear only you.

While this prayer pleases me, I suddenly realize that it, like all my prayers, is utterly selfish. I'd spent precious little time praying for the healing of others' pain, the granting of others' intentions. Occasionally a gruesome news story about violence inflicted upon a child moves me to pray for that child. Or memories of my father, my sister Kim, or my grandmother Sally lead me to pray for them. But on the whole my prayers are seldom for others. Praying for my children doesn't count because they still feel like a part of me even though I know they are my guests and not my possessions.

I challenged myself to move outward in my prayer.

The Other Prayer

> Lord, grant
> all those you love
> the benefit of my prayers.
> Let their pain and need
> and want move me
> more than my own.
> Though they be other
> let them be one with me
> as we are one with you.
> Bestow the gifts they seek,
> the grace they've been
> stranger to, the blessings
> I once asked for myself.
> Allow us all to be other-wise.

Dinner is less lively than usual, in keeping with the slowness of the day. My tomato cantaloupe soup is a great success, and I eat two pieces of Lillian's coconut cake. After dinner I practice writing by candlelight with my left hand, an exercise that is supposed to promote creativity and cross-lateral thinking.

Then I snuff the candle and go out to pay homage to the stars. I listen to the stillness and discover how much there is to hear in what now passes for quiet. I wonder what it must have been like to listen at night before there were cars or planes or electricity to keep the world humming past lights out.

I'd darkened Thomas so no reflected light would obscure my view of the sky. When I rise to go back in, I discover that I hadn't completely closed the screen door. There's a rather substantial gap. I hope no bugs have gotten in. I cross the tile floor to the lamp and click it on.

To my horror, a scorpion is inside. Its tail rises as it registers the bright light and my presence. I pretend not to see the scorpion, but pick up a thick book from my desk and casually cross the room. I hope that if I act nonchalant it will think I haven't seen it and stay still. Just as I draw even with the scorpion, I let the heavy volume fall flat from my left hand right on top of the scorpion. Only then do I let myself get close.

There is no movement from the sides of the book, no evidence of the scorpion anywhere. After a few minutes, I gather the courage to move the book. The pale yellow scorpion looks perfectly flat, the way the petals of a rose pressed in a Bible might look. All its parts are intact but rendered nearly one-dimensional as though they were merely an illustration of a scorpion. An inky puddle of ooze that had been scorpion blood or venom leaks from both sides of the hook-shaped tail.

Next to the hapless scorpion lies my weapon — a hardcover book titled *Desert Life*. I snap a Polaroid to capture the irony and to show my son that I was brave enough to kill a formidable and poisonous insect. But what would Francis of Assisi have done? It now occurs to me that the lowly scorpion qualifies as "the least of my little ones" and that I have somehow violated nature, if not a commandment.

I remember when I was a teenager and we'd had a small infestation of field mice in our house. My father refused to kill the mice because he said they were cute. He'd befriended one who used to come down the stairs to breakfast with him. I was angry with my father for not getting rid of what I thought were unsanitary pests. So one night I secretly set mousetraps in big paper grocery bags all over the house. In the morning when I checked the bags it was as though our first floor were a war zone. There was mouse carnage everywhere. My father was angry, and even though I believed I'd done the right thing I felt bad.

That's how I feel tonight. I feel like a killer, not a composer of prayers.

Hermit

I prepare to say good-bye to Thomas and move to Bede.

I wash the floors, scrub the sink and toilet, polish the mirror, dust the furniture, wash and replace the linens. I had hoped through mindfulness and being in a spiritual community I would learn to relish these tasks, but the experience just reinforces my inclination to put them off as long as possible at home.

When I move into Bede I feel like a first-time home-owner. This place is mine. I open all the blinds so I can enjoy the south, north, and west views. My desk faces west, toward the mountains and sunset. My bed is against the north wall and faces the fox-feeding area to the south. Bede has a little galley kitchen with a compact refrigerator, a Mr. Coffee, and a mix and match collection of silverware, cups, bowls, and plates. There is even a microwave and some glass cooking dishes and utensils. I don't have to take breakfast with the group anymore if I don't want to.

Just to the west of Bede is my own private entrance to the wash, a new way to take my hike from the back way and enjoy the views in reverse, to see the trail as though it were new. I want to take it now, and I do.

It's a short, fast hike. Today I'm scheduled for spiritual guidance with Father Kane and don't want to miss my appointment.

After purifying myself of desert dust I set out for his office.

I find it next to the library. All the walls are covered with books. He is sitting behind his desk. There is an old-fashioned typewriter and a computer so Father Kane can live in two eras of the material world as well as in the spiritual world. Father Kane is about my height, five feet eight and portly. He has white hair, a white beard, and piercingly blue eyes behind his glasses. He's in his eighties, has survived a bout with cancer, and is facing angioplasty. His countenance is untroubled, almost merry. He would be a perfect Santa Claus if not for the undeniable aura of holiness that emanates from him.

He asks if I have been on many retreats, and I tell him this is my first one. He says he is surprised, as I seem like an old hand at this. I don't mention the many years I spent living alone.

"What is it you would like to talk about?" he asks.

His clear eyes are so all-seeing that I must look away.

"I came here to write, but now all I want to do is read. I read eighteen books my first nine days here, and I still need to read more."

"What have you been reading?"

I tell him about Evelyn Underwood, Simon Tugwell, and the rest.

"I'm surprised you haven't been reading Merton."

"I read a lot of Merton when I was younger, but now, for some reason, what he writes no longer touches me."

He asks me about myself: "Are you married, do you have children?" I tell him about Jim, Fabiana, Viveca, and Julian.

"Your children are six, eight, and nine? Well, no wonder you want to read. You probably haven't read much in the last nine years."

I laugh.

"Your busy family life is probably why Merton's cloistered existence no longer speaks to you. But I would recommend you go back and read his first book, *The Seven Storey Mountain*, and also a splendid new biography of him that is just coming out."

He went on. "Of the reading you've done, what do you like best?"

I reply that I am sexist and prefer the company of women, especially Annie Dillard and Kathleen Norris.

"Ah," Father Kane says. "There is so much wonderful writing by women these days. I'm not surprised."

I am surprised, though, by his very open and quite feminist orientation.

"Would you like me to recommend some additional reading?"

"Yes, please." I take notes as he quickly rattles off a ream of titles.

"If you like Kathleen Norris, get *Falling Off, The Middle of the World,* and *Little Girls in Church*. You mentioned Hildegard of Bingen, and if you like her I would also read Mechtild, Mary of Egypt, and St. Scholastica. Evelyn Waugh's *Acedia* is brilliant."

"You like Simon Tugwell?" he asked. "Do some reading about *Point Vierge* and the practice of *lectio,* or spiritual reading."

He pauses for a moment. "St. Thérèse of Lisieux. She said, 'Perfection consists in being what God wants us to be.' A good thought for you to ponder. She also has much to say about the ability to live in uncertainty, what is called negative capability. You'd find that interesting."

I jot down his recommendations furiously. Father Kane goes on to mention Robert Coles's *The Spiritual Life of Children,* Pseudo Macarius, Evagrius, John Climacus, and Benedicta Ward.

"That should be enough to keep you busy for now," he concluded. "By the way, what is it you are writing?"

I tell him that I thought I was writing a book of prayers, but now it seems like hubris for such an imperfect being as myself to presume to write prayers for anyone.

He ponders this for a while. We sit in silence. Then he says, "What is wrong with a sinner writing prayers for the rest of us sinners? The world needs more prayers written by mothers and fathers, by people balancing jobs and children and still hungering for spiritual life and growth. Maybe the reason you feel distant from Thomas Merton now is the reason so many everyday people feel a spiritual life is impractical for them. Write your prayers and see whether they speak to people."

After another pause he asks what made me decide to come here. I tell him about *Six Months Off,* the book in which I'd first read about Desert House, and give an abbreviated account of the abrupt end of my twenty-four years in advertising. He notes that more and more people are turning to the spiritual realm after successful careers in the world. He says that now more middle-aged men than eighteen-year-olds enter the priesthood and the same is true for women's religious orders.

He looks at me and my true issue emerges. "I have trouble believing that God forgives me for some terrible sins I have committed. I had an abortion. I've gone through a ceremony where you write your sin on paper and it is burned as an offering to God and you are supposed to then feel forgiven. I don't. Nothing works."

I realize that I have just gone to confession for the first time in fifteen or twenty years. And not behind a curtain or a screen, but face-to-face.

Father Kane does not seem horrified by my blurt. It is not too much intimacy for him to handle. Maybe he's heard worse.

"Remember when I talked on Sunday about the power of the mantra? 'God loves me' has proven time after time to be the most powerful belief you can hold. I want you to take this as your mantra, and over time you will come to believe it. Because God does love you and forgive you. Benedicta Ward says that 'for all sins there is forgiveness. What really lies outside the ascetic life is despair, the proud attitude that denies the possibility of forgiveness.' Do not despair. God loves you."

I am crying now and have to use a tissue.

Father Kane gets a twinkle in his eye. "Besides, you have work to do. It's time for you to go from advertising to advertising God."

I smile. The last thirty minutes have been so rich. They have covered the last forty years, and probably the next forty. I feel unbearably light when I step out into the sun, the foreshadowing of what it might be like to have a glorified body. I fly through the rest of the day, high on the possibility of God's love and forgiveness. Later, back at Bede, I write my own Mass which I call "Mass for One." My prayers are gaining a lightness of being, too. Despite my best efforts to write from darkness, I find myself too hopeful to bemoan my fate. Before sleep I pray for new gifts.

Dona Nobis Pacem

Lord, give me your peace:
The peace of the womb,
The sleep of the just,
The clarity of the committed,
The eyes of the guileless,
The content past desire. Amen.

Amatole Polis

Patsy, Nick, and I are in Nick's car heading south for our mission hop. First stop is San Xavier del Bac, a mission established by the Franciscan Padre Eusebio Francisco Kino in 1692.

You can see San Xavier many miles before you reach it. Its huge domes are supernaturally white against the cloudless blue sky and distant dusty brown mountains. Nick says it is called The White Dove of the Desert. The mission's church does have the look of a white bird with spread wings since a white dome rises on each side of the church's core.

I am startled to find that the statues of saints inside the church are clothed, which makes them seem like big dolls. I imagine that it must have been fun for the young women of the Papago tribe to sew the elaborate costumes for these saints and then dress them, a sanctioned break from their long work days to "play" under the auspices of the church and the blessings of God himself.

San Xavier wears black and white clerical garb when depicted as alive. But at his shrine in a side chapel where he is dead, he is covered with a bright blue satin coverlet edged in lace, as though death's glorified body would also require a more flamboyant and lively form of raiment.

The statue of Jesus in the Chapel of the Suffering Savior wears red satin, the color of kingship and blood. The crown on his head is made of real thorns.

Our Sorrowful Mother, ensconced in her own chapel, wears a light blue satin ballgown and a lace mantilla.

This practice of clothing statues originated in Spain. I like it because it instantly makes the statues more human, capable of being tempted, lonely, joyful, loved. I believe this Jesus and this Mary might forgive my sins.

I light two candles — one at the side chapel holding the sorrowful mother and one at St. Xavier's shrine. The first candle I light for the love and health of Jim and me and the children; the other candle is in supplication for Jim's business and a new direction for whatever gifts I might possess.

I notice tiny metal legs pinned to San Xavier's blue satin coverlet. Pictures of children are pinned there, too. Apparently, Xavier is credited with miracles of healing.

Those whom he has healed pin the part of the body he has helped to the coverlet.

I tell Patsy I feel guilty about having missed this morning's Mass. "Why?" she asks. "It's good to vary your routine once in a while."

Later she says, "Most human misery occurs because people don't feel God loves them." It's as though she sensed the direction of my session with Father Kane. She is supposed to be resting and on retreat, too, but finds herself acting as an informal spiritual director for many of us. Her lessons spring from who she is and the teaching moments that present themselves. Just before our trip she gave me an article on Catherine of Siena and the gift of discernment because she knew I'd just begun reading Catherine and had been doing some similar reading herself. Maybe we are all acting as each other's spiritual directors.

Nick points out that in the bas relief above the church's entrance there are two small animal figures: a cat and a mouse. He says that it is believed that when this cat catches this mouse it will signal the end of the world.

Our next stop is the church of San Cayetano de Tumacacori on the banks of the now dry Santa Cruz River. It is part of the larger Tumacacori National Monument, which preserves part of the historical Gadsden Purchase from Spain in 1853.

In the church's courtyard is an old graveyard. The last person buried there, in 1916, was an infant Pima Indian girl. Her grave is raised and covered in pink stone, like a frosted birthday cake. There is an arbor where the headstone would be, with a wreath of dried pink flowers.

There are no statues here, clothed or otherwise. They have all been stolen. What do you do when all your heroes, your saints, have been stolen from you?

These missions feel like monuments to hope in what has been an exceptionally violent history. Their hope still fills me, even though now the greatest immediate danger is from falling prey to the temptations of the gift shops. It is important to build structures that soar because they do lift those who enter them.

We cross the border into Nogales, but I am not really there. The contrast between the purity of The White Dove and the trinketry of this city is just too great. The worms in the tequila bottles threaten. I want to go back to Bede. I want to go back to my children. I have had enough of being a tourist, spiritual or otherwise. Patsy and Nick talk quietly all the way home, but I say nothing. I'm just along for the ride.

It's dinnertime. On the side table in the common room I am excited to see I have several pieces of mail. One is a FedEx package from Jim and our babies. The other is a letter with no postmark or address, just my name. When I open it, there is a beautiful card and bookmark from Sister Jeanne, who had to return home today.

I am sorry to have missed Jeanne. I really enjoyed our walks to the face in the tree and our discussions about art and life at dinner. The card inside her envelope bears a logo design she created. Inside the card is an explanation of the symbology. At the top of the card it says "Jesus Christ: Yesterday, Today and Forever." The chi rho (the letters χ and ρ, which are the Greek letters for Christos) are the central elements, combined with a circle representing the rising, setting, and full-noon sun. It stands for wholeness and endless movement. Sister Jeanne has put a great deal of thought and history into her design, and I am honored by this gift of her gift.

Back at Bede I open the sheaf of photocopied pages Sister Patsy gave me on St. Catherine of Siena and the gift of discernment.

Catherine lived in Siena, Italy, from 1347 to 1380 during the time of the Black Death and the constant warfare waged by mercenary armies on behalf of their client city-states. Rome had become so dangerous that the pope had moved to Avignon, France, and left the administration of the church's business to corrupt and arrogant legates. So Catherine was born into a kind of wilderness nearly as forbidding as that of the desert.

She was the twenty-fourth of twenty-five children. In the time of the Black Death it was wise to have as many children as you could afford since one never knew when one or many might be snatched from you. Death was all around. Her prosperous parents hoped she would make an advantageous marriage, but Catherine told them she wanted to be a bride of Christ, and to convince them of her seriousness she cut off all her beautiful blond hair. As punishment for this defilement of her own beauty, her parents relegated her to the status of a servant. To keep her sanity, Catherine constructed a safe interior world, what she called her "secret cell," to which she could retreat at any time during her long, hard work days. In this cell she could live in peace with Christ even though the rest of her life was controlled by the desires of others.

Once when Catherine knelt in prayer, her father saw a dove fluttering over her head. This vision convinced her father to let her pursue her vocation. But instead of joining a formal religious order, she became a Dominican *mantellata*. (The *mantellate* were a group of widows who worked with the sick and poor in Siena.) For three years she stayed in her room, a cell with four walls that had replaced the one in her head. She was tormented

146

by doubts, demons, and taunting until she finally ended their assault with her own laughter. After this difficult period she was blessed by daily visitations by Christ. During one of his visits she said she saw him place a ring on her finger. She was finally married to the one man she loved.

After her marriage she emerged from seclusion to live a life of service to the sick, the poor, the imprisoned, and the victimized. Her holiness and several healings attributed to her gained her many followers, both men and women, who called themselves "Caterinata" and called her "Mamma." She also became an adept mediator of temporal conflicts between families and city-states, intervening most notably in the feud between Florence and Avignon. Catherine visited the exiled Pope Gregory XI and convinced him to leave the corruption of Avignon's court and return to Rome, which he did.

This did not lead to the reemergence of an uncorrupt church hierarchy as had been her hope. Gregory's death led to the rise of two rival popes, who conducted wars against each other for several decades. Catherine had prayed to God that she be allowed to atone for the sins of the church. Shortly after this she collapsed in pain, became paralyzed, and soon died. Her body bore the marks of the stigmata and a visible ring where Christ's invisible wedding band had once been placed.

How palpable her holiness must have been that even the misogynistic church fathers and their faithful put their trust in her. Hers was a holiness that overcame all objections and all dissension. No wonder she was such a successful mediator. She could discern the truth of any situation and act appropriately. To most of us, this would be the ultimate gift. It would be a way to live in our own personal wilderness with all its temptations and confusions and still keep our integrity.

How does one cultivate the quality of discernment? First one has to understand what discernment really is. It is more than the simple ability to tell right from wrong. In Catherine's view, it is the capacity to recognize and carry out the truly good. She was able to perceive the higher good to be pursued in any situation, and her great capacity for giving let her act on that perception. So discernment is really two qualities: wisdom and charity. "It is a virtue based on the knowledge of self acquired in prayer." In her book *The Dialogue,* Catherine talks about how the more a person comes to know the truth about God and herself, the more she seeks to become transformed into "another Christ." And as she grows in union with God, her desire becomes the key to "see" and choose what is truly the highest good.

Catherine advises those who would seek to grow in this gift to do so by "going into the cell of self-knowledge" and attending to inner experience. Attending to inner experience is a part of her practice of continuous prayer. This is how we gain knowledge of God. There are two parts to knowledge of God: the felt experience of knowing how much God loves us and the feeling that we need God.

I have come to feel, with Father Kane's help, that God does love me. In times of pain and suffering I am aware of how much I need God. But that's not the same as knowing one's need for God even when the going isn't so rough. Do I choose prayer and intimacy with God when I feel in control? No. Like most, I attribute my success solely to my own efforts, my own perceived inherent superiority. It's so American to attribute all the good that comes one's way to rugged individualism and pulling one's self up by one's bootstraps. I thank God in some perfunctory way if what happens feels "lucky." I thank others for the small parts (from my limited perspective) they may have played in my good fortune. But that's not the same as knowing that good can't happen without God.

And then there's that thorny question of what really constitutes success. I am so very far from defining success in spiritual terms instead of material ones. The more points I rack up for career advancements, raises, accomplishments, and my own and my children's test scores and awards, the more successful I feel. Every set-back in the same categories feels like loss, even though it might result in greater understanding. Do I really know when I'm successful? And why do I need so much affirmation from others to feel as though I am?

Discernment isn't something one can grasp from such limited reading or even more thorough investigation. It is a gift, and its development is as dependent on whether God thinks you are ready for it as it is on your own effort. I think you have to be ready for this gift because it demands that you act upon what you are graced to see. Not everybody is ready to act. I'm not. I want to be comfortable, and discernment and comfort don't seem likely bedfellows.

From the emptiness I feel in my stomach I discern it's time for dinner. My watch says I can still catch Vespers so I fly from Bede to the Chapel of Our Lady of Solitude.

Following an after-dinner stroll I retreat to Bede for more reading. I'm intrigued by stories of the female desert mystics and want to know how they came to be revered by the men of their faiths when church, synagogue, and mosque hierarchies were then so dominated by men. "Then?" I catch myself on the word. It is now as it was then except for a very few examples.

I'd been drawn to a volume by Benedicta Ward, *Harlots of the Desert*, because the title held the tension of opposites and the great energy they can generate. I'd once given a speech about understanding the tension of opposites in a brand and how they spark interest and emotion in the audience. In a sense a book is a brand, too, and sends its own energy out to potential readers. *Harlots of the Desert* called out to me and I accepted its invitation.

The preface indicates that these are texts of repentance with the same theme as the most powerful Bible stories: the return of everyman to the kingdom that had been lost. The stories of these women, while different in the details, are all about transformation from prostitution to sanctity. These are women I wish I could meet and question: Ammah Sarah, Mary Magdalene, Mary of Egypt, Pelagia, Thais, and Maria, niece of Abraham, who lived lives of freedom from society's limitations and responsibilities both before and during *anachoreisis,* the term for secluded life in the desert.

Ammah Sarah was a lustful hussy who left "the life" (as prostitutes often refer to their profession) to live alone by the Nile for thirteen years. She said that during this time she was constantly tempted by the devil to have lustful thoughts. But it was said of her that "she never prayed that the warfare should cease, but she said, 'O God, give me strength.'" How strong she was not to ask deliverance from bedevilment but strength to fight it instead. She wanted to be honed by these difficult experiences. My prayers always ask for easiness. I am an "easy" woman.

While we generally brand Mary Magdalene as a prostitute, it isn't clear that she really took money for sex. Apparently original texts describe her as *amatole polis,* a "woman of the city," and don't refer to her as *hetaira,* the word for prostitute. Seven devils were driven from her, not just lust. This fits with the monks' conception of prostitution as something we all do whenever we are unfaithful to our covenant with God and spend more time acquiring material goods than we do tending our souls. Perhaps Mary of Magdala was merely a clothes horse who spent her time making herself attractive to men and bedding them; if so, she is not so different from many women of the twenty-first century. She is not dissimilar to me.

Despite her impurity, God chose her to be the first to take news of the Resurrection to the apostles and to anoint Christ for burial and bless his feet with her tears. Impurity is no impediment to salvation if the heart is open to it. Mary was aware of her need for God's mercy as so many of us are not. Ward quotes a poetic passage from Peter Chrysologus about Mary concerning the Day of Resurrection: "On this later day, a woman runs to grace who earlier ran to guilt. She hastens to snatch life from death who had snatched death from life."

Long after Mary Magdalene's death and her burial in Aix en Provence, France, she became the object of fanatical devotion almost as intense as that for the Virgin Mary. In the twelfth century her relics were traded, sold, and stolen, and fragments of her body were given as gifts to highly placed men all over Europe. A priest chopped off her arm and displayed it as his possession. It is ironic that the church treated her body like a high-priced call girl's even while it asserted its veneration of her holiness. She was treated in death as she had been in her earlier life.

Mary of Egypt lived a dissolute life in Alexandria and professed she had sex just for the fun of it and not for money. One day on a whim she joined a group of religious pilgrims headed for Jerusalem by ship. She accompanied them to the Church of the Holy Sepulchre. They all went in, but when she tried to follow them she was stopped at the threshold by an invisible force that would not let her in. That night she was filled with sincere contrition for all her sins. In the morning when she sought to enter the church, the force did not prevent her and she was able to venerate the relic of the true cross inside.

After this experience she lived by herself in the desert for forty-seven years until her death. She told the holy man Zossima that throughout these years she was tortured by strong desires for fish, meat, and the sweet wine she once swilled in Alexandria. The devil also made her remember lewd songs she had sung in her youth. When she died, Zossima said a lion helped him dig her grave.

Mary probably never thought of herself as holy because she could not escape temptation but only fight it as best she could, like an alcoholic tackling her addiction, drinkless day by drinkless day, and never being able to say "I'm not an alcoholic anymore." None of us will ever stop being sinners until we die. All we can do is try not to slip into sin in the hundreds of moments of weakness that present themselves every day.

Pelagia was the greatest actress in the ancient city of Antioch, who "dressed in the height of fantasy, wearing nothing but gold, pearls and precious stones." Her affinity for jewels led her to be called Margaret among her admirers because it meant "pearl." At the time the church fathers regarded actresses as part of a class of immoral persons that included jesters, mimics, jugglers, and clowns.

Nonnus, the bishop of Antioch, was so struck by Pelagia's beauty the first time he saw her that it was as though he had fallen in love. He channeled that love not into lust but into passionately praying for her soul all that night. The next day she heard him preaching and was drawn to his voice as though mesmerized. His words moved her to repentance and she was later baptized by Nonnus. Immediately afterward she disguised herself in men's clothing and fled to Palestine. Years later Nonnus asked James the Deacon to visit a hermit in Palestine called Pelagius. When James arrived he realized that Pelagius was the Pelagia who once was a flagrant libertine. By then she was revered for her holy purity and wisdom.

Thais, another of the harlots, was also beautiful, popular, and wealthy, and had so many lovers that they constantly fought over her to win her favor. One day the holy man Paphnutius came to her brothel disguised as a lover and convinced her that her soul was in grave danger and that she must repent. He told her to repeat this prayer as many times as she could: "You who have made me have mercy upon me." Then he left her with a convent of nuns.

Thais came to be seen as the epitome of the person who responds correctly to the gift of grace. She immediately accepted Paphnutius's insight into her state and resolved to change then and there. She didn't mull it over or dismiss him as a lunatic. She also knew that she couldn't trust only herself to do the right thing, so she placed herself in the hands of the holy man and accepted his tutelage in righteousness. Grace is a moment of opportunity; we can either accept it graciously, as did Thais, or lose the moment. Most of us choose to let the moment pass us by. How much easier it is to accept God on one's deathbed or in great illness when we've already had our surfeit of worldly pleasure and it seems we have nothing to lose. Because grace doesn't make things easier; it makes them harder.

The last of Ward's chosen harlots was Maria, the niece of Abraham. She was an orphan whose uncle, Abraham the Monk, brought her up in a home of goodness. But one night she was seduced by a visiting monk and gave in to his charms. Rather than confess her fall to Abraham she fled in guilt and despair to the city, where she made her living as a prostitute. Abraham came to get her and bring her home without remonstration. She returned with him to live a life of repentance.

The stories of these harlots became known widely because they were told again and again by the monks of the sixth century. The monks believed their stories should be heard by all so that the moments of grace in these women's lives would continue to touch others. The monks taught that sin is no barrier to grace, but rather the barrier is the pride that cannot bear to admit that it has fallen and therefore cannot ask for forgiveness of mercy. This is the very failing of which I am most guilty. And because I am unable to ask for mercy, I can't grant it to others. I need others to be sinful and unmercied so my sins don't seem as terrible or my fall as far. I think the monks got it right — pride goeth after a fall.

The monks also told these stories as counterbalance to the tales of the "good" women of the monastic world: Marcella, Eugenia, Macrina, and Melania. These women chose the holy way from the get-go, which is not to dismiss the difficulty of their choices. But they never let themselves fall as far as the harlots did and their exemplariness made it harder for the less ordinary to see lessons for themselves in the holy women's lives.

I close Ward's book but it follows me out into the night. The stars shine like the pearls and diamonds that adorned Pelagia the actress. I hold the stars responsible for making us lust for anything that shines, for the diamonds in our wedding rings, the tiaras of princesses and beauty queens. It's not our fault, God; you made the heavens too beautiful not to want them for our own. You made some people so beautiful it was too hard to just look and not want to touch. Flesh has its own translucence and transcendence. That's why we sing the body electric.

Back in bed I lie without blankets or sheets and make an unholy wish for a big mirror above my bed. Then I could see how I look to the stars as I lay sleeping in their soft light. How I look to God. I want to see what he sees, to know whether I please him. I am no Thais, no Pelagia, but it would make me happy to know he thinks I'm beautiful. And that, of course, is the downfall of any woman. Any *amatole polis*.

A Fallen Woman's Prayer

I didn't all at once plunge into hell.
This is how I fell:
Every day I told one lie,
refused one favor,
seduced one guy.
It didn't seem like much;
tiny missteps, slips and such
that left me just a touch
away from bottom.
A bottom I now press against
with all my might,
muscles tensed in fight-or-flight.
I've got all the strength
of the nearly drowned,
the once were lost and now are found.
I'll surface again:
I can see the light.

Javalina

Despite my disenchantment with yesterday's tourist trek, Patsy and Nick easily break my resolve to keep to myself. Besides, my long hermetic reading stints when we returned to Desert House have acted as an emetic. Nogales and noise have been purged from my system. At lunch they suggest a short trip to the Desert Museum to see a film about the plant and animal life of the desert. How can my soul be sullied by nature study?

I can't imagine any film being as wonderful as the one Nick has described. But he's right. The film has considerable dramatic flair and even a sense of humor. When the film is over, the curtain/screen pulls away revealing a gigantic window through which we see the real life equivalent of what we've just witnessed in the last scene. It is stunning, but proves that live is still better than virtual.

We loop through Cortaro on the way back and stop at a tribal casino. I wonder whether people here like gambling more than those in other parts of the country, because the parking lot is absolutely jammed. When we get inside and feel the air conditioning, I conclude that most of them have probably decided that losing ten or twenty dollars is a small price to pay for such cool comfort.

The garish, insistent lights of the machines, the electronic song of the slots, the steady stream of coinfall in metal and paper cups give me a headache. I have always hated gambling. It robs us not only of money, but of time, focus, thinking, will. It's depressing. I don't even drop a single quarter in a machine. Again, I wish I'd stayed back at Bede with my books. What lesson is to be learned from such poor choices? What am I afraid I'll miss if I don't go? Or am I more afraid of Patsy and Nick thinking I'm not very nice if I choose not to go?

When we get back I need to perform ablutions. I say a rosary, each decade of beads devoted to a different family member. After, it seems the right time to read and meditate about Mary's role in the church and in the prayer life of us ordinary mortals.

The modern-day devotion to Mary is astounding when you consider that Mary herself did nothing to try to secure herself a place in history. She never strove to

accomplish anything of significance; she merely gracefully accepted the blessing and burden of being the
mother of God. She was not a pubic speaker, a writer
of books, a leader of men or women.

I wonder whether any of her contemporaries were
jealous of her status or wished they had been singled
out for greatness. Perhaps some of them sneered at her
unremarkable person and thought "Why her? She's no
better than me. Why didn't God pick me?" Certainly
she would be envied today, when everyone seems to be
vying for their personal fifteen minutes of fame and the
chance to be featured in *People* or *Us.*

It's hard to imagine Mary enjoying the limelight. She
was always there, but ever in the background, like a
presidential aide who participates in history without
once being a subject for a photo op.

It's also hard to imagine Mary feeling deserving of
her selection as a temple of God, his house. And how
could she not marvel at the irony of her nurturing and
raising God to be a good person? After all, she knew
who he was and was destined to be. I wonder whether
she ever doubted her anointment or his calling, whether
she felt her mind had played tricks on her and that she
might be going insane.

But self-doubt seems such a modern phenomenon,
the product of a time that insists that only the rational

is valid, blocking out our ability to hear the instinctive and the sacred.

Self-doubt must visit those in this century who've been privileged to witness one of Mary's apparitions. There is no scientific explanation for these phenomena. And yet in the last sixty years alone, there have been more than two hundred sightings, more than in the whole of the nineteenth century. What is the Mary of Medjugorje and Fatima and Lourdes trying to tell us? Does she appear more often now because we are slow to decipher her message, slower than people in simpler times? Perhaps she has learned what those of us who create television commercials know: you must repeat, repeat, repeat to get your message across.

I keep thinking about Mary and how to talk to her. I find it easier to talk to her son because in a strange way he seems more human. The only role she plays that I can relate to is mother. But she is the Mother of God! She's royalty. And still a virgin. I would be much more comfortable talking to Mary Magdalene or Mary of Egypt. But they were never mothers, at least as far as the literature indicates.

I wonder whether Mary punished Jesus because he talked back to her or came home late or stole candy at the market. Was she the one who talked to him about the birds and the bees or did she leave that to Joseph? What if he didn't keep his room clean or she didn't like his friends? Did she ever scream or threaten or make sarcastic comments? Probably not. But I would like to think that like the harlots of the desert she at least thought about it before deciding not to. As with the desert monastics, I value more the lessons of sinners who choose to do good than those who have never been tempted.

I don't think I'd like being around Mary very much. She doesn't seem to have had a sense of humor or an appreciation of irony, as portrayed by church fathers. I sometimes get the feeling she wasn't very bright. Blasphemy! Luciferian! I know that goodness is more important than intelligence, and I'm not a supporter of the meritocracy's new order. Still, one would hope for a little more dimension in the being chosen to be the mother of God.

I say another rosary after dinner while I walk the Stations of the Cross in the day's most heavenly light. This one is for me and for all mothers who need someone to talk to about the hardest job in the world. Then I ask Mary to forgive me my insulting thoughts. She understands. Sometimes she wishes she weren't quite so perfect. Being on a pedestal is so lonely it hurts almost as much as a crown of thorns.

Back at Bede I'm ready for another round of reading. I want to know more about women mystics of other faiths. This seems in the ecumenical spirit of Bede Griffiths who went to India and the Hindus to find, as he put it, "the other half of my soul."

In Margaret Smith's *Muslim Women Mystics* I learn of Rabi'a of Basra and other female Muslim mystics who were revered by the Muslim men of their time, around the late eighth century AD or the first century AH.

Rabi'a was a Sufi mystic and saint born in poverty in Basra about AH 95 or 99 (AD 717). Her name means "the fourth" because she was her parents' fourth daughter. They were so poor that they had no oil in their house to light a lamp nor swaddling clothes to wrap her in the night she was born. Her father wouldn't even borrow from his neighbors because he had made a Sufi vow that he would never ask anything of a creature and depend on God alone to supply his needs. That night her father dreamt that the prophet Mohammed appeared to him and said, "Do not be sorrowful, for this daughter who is born is a great saint." Mohammed also instructed him to send a letter to the amir, or ruler of Basra, reminding him that he was to say four hundred prayers to Mohammed on Friday nights and that because he neglected to do so he must pay Rabi'a's father four hundred dinars. Her father did as instructed and the family was provided for as Mohammed prophesied.

But soon after her parents died and Rabi'a was left an orphan, a famine visited Basra and she was separated from her sisters. An evil man kidnapped her and sold her as a slave to another man who worked her very hard. One day her master saw a halo around her while she prayed and was frightened so he set her free. She went at once into the desert, at first making a living as a flute, player and then she later sequestered herself in a cell where she devoted her days to prayer and works of piety. A renowned ascetic and theologian proposed to her but she rejected his offer as sensual and chose a celibate path. She also rejected offers from the Amir and the governor, saying that it would not please her to be distracted from God for even a moment.

Much of her story parallels the stories of Christian women mystics and their turning away from the charms of the world. But like them, in this turning away she also secured for herself a freedom few women of the time enjoyed. She had many male friends with temporal and spiritual power who treated her as an equal and sometimes as their better since they sought her counsel and wisdom on the highest matters.

At night she said this prayer from her desert rooftop, which acted as a ritual opening for other prayers and verses appropriate for the close of the day: "O my Lord, the stars are shining and the eyes of men are closed, and kings have shut their doors and every lover is alone with his beloved, and here I am alone with Thee."

So there was something of the sensualist in Rabi'a after all. She loves her God as the female Christian mystics often do, as the harlots did, as the perfect lover and bridegroom.

Rabi'a seemed to have the gift of discernment that Catherine of Siena possessed, too, for she prayed as one suffused by love and charity and therefore perception: "O my Lord, whatever share of this world Thou dost bestow on me, bestow it on Thine enemies, and whatever share of the next world Thou dost give me, give it to Thy friends. Thou art enough for me."

Rabi'a lived until she was nearly ninety, but despite her goodness, like most Sufis she feared death and its attendant judgment by the Lord because to be found sinful was to risk separation from God forever. That was why when others asked her what she most desired, she would say it was death because she felt that for every day she lived she was more likely to commit sins that might lead to such separation. She finally did meet death in AH 185 (AD 801). It's time to sleep. I find Rabi'a's night prayer and say it. I'm too tired to write one of my own.

In the middle of the night I smell something so foul it wakes me from deep sleep. The smell is funky, sharp as blue cheese, and violating as a fart. It is a sinister odor, like that of a corpse dug up by a grave robber.

I'd left the sliding glass doors open with only the screens to separate me from the outside so I could hear the foxes when they came to feed. Instead I hear snorts and pushing and sounds I imagine are those of teeth on bone and ligature. My heart beats like it's a machine in a stamping plant, heavy and fast. There must be imprints all over the inside of my chest wall. I put on my glasses and move over enough in the bed to see if I can spy who's out there.

It's a herd of javalinas, desert boars with long snouts, wiry gray fur and small stealthy eyes. They must be the source of the death smell. Kate told me you could usually smell javalinas before you saw them. They aren't eating a baby fox or a desert mouse or a nest of quail as I'd feared. They're chomping into the green stems of cacti around the clay water dish just outside my porch.

I crawl out of bed and move closer. One of the javalinas eyes me coldly and without fear. I am afraid of a javalina who can look at me like this. Then the others follow suit and stare me down, too. I want to look away but I can't. What if they try to rush me in a pack? What if they are like their pig cousins who will crush anyone who makes the mistake of getting in their pen? After all, I am crashing their party and threatening their meal. They head toward the door. I slam the sliding glass doors shut, draw the shades and put out the porch light as though I am closing the house to trick or treaters on Halloween because I have no more candy. Go away, javalinas, there's nothing for you here.

They bounce off each other and Bede like billiard balls against bumpers as they mill around looking for more succulents. The tempo slows and then the sounds fade out. When I'm sure the javalinas are all gone. I get up, carefully open the door, and sniff. The smell is gone.

Now wide awake, I write a prayer. Once it's done I am ready again for dreams. Or nightmares.

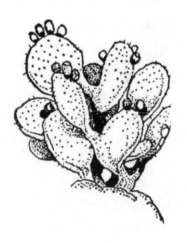

Past Prayer

I'm a woman with a past
and so the last
to have the right
to ask so much of You.
Erase that past
so that I might start anew
and begin to lead the life
that might have been
had I not given in
to every wile and whim:
what the pure of past
call Sin.

Story Hours

It's cloudy when I get up, the first real clouds I've seen since leaving Chicago. I'm late getting up because the light is flat and doesn't send any intrusive rays to rouse me.

A good morning to skip meditation and write.

At dinner the night before I'd joked with Father Kane about how Desert House needed a pool and that I'd be more than glad to make a contribution to such a fund. I told him that the pool could double as a baptismal font, in case the pool on its own seemed too indulgent and removed from the religious mission of a house of prayer. I was still thinking about pools when I woke up, and began writing a story I hadn't intended to write titled "Pool." It is about a retired woman looking for action at a motel in Florida. One of the pre-desert harlots has taken up residence in my brain.

In writing classes I'd only been able to write what I knew, semiautobiographical pieces rooted in my early family experiences. Here at Desert House I am beginning to write about characters who aren't like me or even like anyone I know. They are outside the quagmire of self. It isn't complaint fiction, to borrow from the term "complaint rock" used to characterize angst-ridden alternative music from the Pacific Northwest. It is otherly. Maybe praying more for others is already having an effect.

I don't feel the least bit angsty or even antsy. I am secure in my feelings, instinctive in my hiking, sure that the role of searcher I'm playing is one God has cast me in. I am content to live in negative capability. And intent on making my last two and a half days at Desert House count. No more distractions or side trips no matter how alluring the destination or seductive the company.

But three hours of post-breakfast hiking in the mountains burns up my reserves of positive energy and leaves me feeling depleted and ruminative, a good prospective target for the noonday demon. After lunch I slouch off to Bede. I feel a presence there with me. The dreaded Demon Acedia has dropped in.

The blinds are drawn against the light, and I open them to drive the shadows out. But it's too hot with them open. I close the slats tight, and the demon sinks back in the recliner, comfortable again.

Next I try water. Maybe I am just dehydrated. I pour glass after glass of ice water from the little refrigerator and feel it course through me like the Colorado River through a canyon. I think it's carving new turns in my veins. Blessed water. Blessed but not holy enough to exorcise my unwelcome visitor. The demon pulls the little handle on the recliner's side to the fully horizontal position. Acedia has settled in for the afternoon.

I spend an hour at my desk charting the happiest and saddest years of my life, trying to divine a pattern. The cataloguing and charting make me feel less vulnerable to the demon sitting there in the recliner trying his utmost to mire me in the muck of my past. I discover one very good thing: the older I get, the happier I get, with the exception of the feelings I have about my abortion.

I feel such a sense of loss because I'd longed to keep the baby, to be a mother, to be responsible for someone other than myself. But I'd never had the strength to resist pressure, from boyfriends or parents or peers, and all other opinions about whether I should keep the baby were stacked so completely against mine that I doubted my own judgment. I'd never made a practical plan to take care of the baby so there was nothing to outweigh the overwhelming rationality of the cases those close to me made. I became fearful about my capacity to meet the needs of a baby and took the only path that would stop the madness and give me immediate peace, not knowing that I'd never escape the burden of guilt my abortion would set in place.

Much later, I'd written to a friend's pregnant single daughter that she shouldn't keep her baby, that she should let her mother's and boyfriend's and society's opinions prevail and either give up the baby for adoption or have an abortion. I guess I'd convinced myself that despite the sense of loss and grief, it must have been the right thing to do. She never replied to my letter, but she kept her baby and ignored my unholy advice. I think she recognized lies when she saw them.

Sometimes I envy her. I envy her because she does not have this blot on her soul and can't be harrowed by this demon.

Then I realize that the way to banish the Demon Acedia is to turn to thoughts of other people: their needs, their disappointments, their regrets. In short, their stories. They have so much to say that I need to hear. There are others right here in the room with me ready to tell their stories right now. My battalion of books calls me to open them. They are more than ready for combat with Acedia.

The book with the most insistent voice is one by Lawrence Kushner: *God Was in This Place and I Did Not Know*. It holds the stories of rebbes past eager to dispense their wisdom. The first story I read is that of Rabbi Rashi, a teacher of mid-eleventh-century France who advocated close reading of scripture and close observation of people and events. One passage contains some of the simplest and best advice I've ever heard: "When you look closely and for a long time, you discover things that are invisible to others. Most people make the mistake of trying to 'look deeper' when all they need is to pay attention to the obvious."

There is a story about a woman rebbe, too — Hannah Rachel Werbermacher of Ludomir in the Ukraine, sometimes called "The Maid of Ludomir." She had a religious conversion after a serious illness (why does it always take suffering to make us seek or see God?) and began to acquire and speak wisdom so great that many men came to see her. Actually, by religious law they couldn't look at her. So she would leave the door to her study half open so they could hear her but not break the rules. She believed that good was everywhere, even in the midst of evil, and she admonished those who came to hear her not to let their hearts harden to those whom they judged to be wicked. She advised them not to turn away from evil but to instead turn evil into good.

Turning evil into good. Isn't that what I'm doing with the Demon Acedia? He has become an occasion for me to delve deeper into the very truths he so desperately doesn't want me to access.

I turn to Demon Acedia and smile. "Stay awhile," I say. "You make me want to read."

What book's call to answer next?

Monica Furlong's *Visions and Longings,* a book about medieval women mystics, is the volume I pull from the shelf. I flip quickly to her section on Julian of Norwich to see whether I can supplement my meager knowledge of her. Like the Maid of Ludomir she also believes that God is in everything, even what we judge in our incomplete knowledge to be evil. Julian said, "Oh, wretched sin . . . when I saw that God had made everything I did not see you."

It must pain God that we cannot see the world as it is, that we continue to think in simpleton fashion and divide creation into dualities. Black or white, good or evil, masculine or feminine. Our way of seeing is a part of the truth but it isn't the whole. It's the "or" that gets us into trouble. Julian is able to see in much larger and more divine terms; she talks about Jesus as a mother! "Our precious Mother Christ," she addresses her. Christ is both male and female.

When I read more of Julian I run across a passage that I'm sure I was meant to encounter. It is a prescription for what ails me. "God showed me two kinds of sickness that we have of which he wants us to be cured. One is impatience. because we bear our labor and our pain heavily. The other is despair, coming from doubt and fear."

I pray to be delivered of these twin maladies. And then I feel the atmosphere in my cell lighten. Acedia has gone away to visit someone more attentive to her guest.

It's time for Vespers and dinner now. It's a rhythm of the hours even my reading respects. I always seem to finish in time to keep the schedule. I am as regular as the sun and the moon.

At dinner I learn there will be another story to hear this evening. Dwight will tell the story of his bicycle trip around the periphery of the continental United States and show us his slides. I'm not especially enthusiastic about sitting through a slide show, but this afternoon has convinced me how important it is to hear the stories of others. They can be a form of grace for both the listener and the teller. The sixth-century monks believed this, which is why they repeated the stories of the harlots of the desert and the Desert Fathers over and over again to any who would take the time to hear.

Dwight had been a professor of natural science at the University of Colorado and shared a love of nature and outdoor activity with his first wife. Dwight's wife sparked to his idea of biking the outer edges of the country and carefully plotted out his trip with him. He started his journey ten years ago, but just three months into it his wife died and he returned home. Six months later he resumed his trek with firm resolve to go the distance in his wife's memory and then write a book about it. He did go the distance and is now at Desert House with his second wife to complete a manuscript. They have been living in a hermitage trailer for nearly a year.

The slides he clicks through as he tells his tale are nearly professional in their use of light and framing and vividly illustrate how far he went in pursuit of his dream.

His is a wonderful story even if it never gets published, and I'm glad I came to hear him. I wonder whether I've missed other important stories along the way because I was always too busy to listen to anything that didn't directly bear on the task at hand. Of course I stopped to hear or read the stories of the rich, the infamous, and the powerful. And I often read the well-crafted stories of fictional characters from the pages of best-selling authors. But did I have time for stories from my seatmate on the plane? No. I'd cocoon myself in a silent world circumscribed by the arms of my own seat. Did I have time for the Jobean tales of woe and sickness told by older family members? No. I didn't want them to interrupt the news or the dialogue of a movie.

It's always easy to dismiss a story out of hand because you don't hold the teller in awe. Yet these neglected stories could be far more pertinent than the ones I chose to listen, and I would never know it. I would never know what I lost because I failed to recognize these stories as gifts. As grace.

Dwight also made me confront my own ageism. Here I was, just across the dividing line into the dread demographic category of "45 to 54," unable to accept that I was middle-aged and getting older. I had been dismissive of Dwight because he was sixty-four, and I had assumed that his faculties were fading, that he would ramble and lose the through-line in his narrative, that his observations wouldn't be keen. What did this say about my professed desire to get in touch with the eternal? What about my resentment of the youthism of advertising? Why was I so blind to my own prejudices concerning age and worth? Maybe putting distance between Dwight and myself was my own automatic defense weapon against being put in the "old" category. If I thought he was old then how could anyone think I was old?

It's late when I get back to Bede, later than I had hoped. In the back of my mind I had thought I would duck out of Dwight's show early and slip away unspotted to enjoy some private time on my next-to-last night. But I didn't and now it's nearly nine o'clock, late by retreat standards.

I say another rosary of dedicated decades. Today Grandma Sally, my sister Kim, Fabiana, Viveca, and Julian are the beneficiaries of my efforts at otherful prayer. I don't know why I pray for Sally and Kim; I am sure they are in heaven and can't imagine why they would be made to suffer more than they already had. But I don't want to be presumptuous and leave them out just in case they do need prayer.

Now it's nine thirty. I missed the fox visit, but they had been here. Half-eaten apples presented evidence. I hope the javalinas don't come again because they scare me, although I've come to be more sympathetic to them and their smell since I've learned they don't see well and use smell to find their way back to the pack. The lonely sounds of the desert fill the long intervals between cars on Picture Rocks Road as I write at my desk.

Prayer for Insight

God, let me see what I can't feel
and feel what I can't see.
Let me know another's pain
and see the truth within.
Show me what my eyes have missed;
let me hear what I dismissed.
Make me worthy of your greatest gift:
to see what is and what could be.

Day Fourteen / Friday

Rain

I awaken earlier than usual, courtesy of my neglected but unvengeful alarm clock. It's 5:00 a.m. and the sun is just beginning to stir. I am mindful that this is my last full day at Desert House and am determined to make the most of it.

I set off on my hike at once because I've been told that it's easier to spot animals in the early dawn. I wear my blue rosary to ward off evil and carry twice as much water as usual.

Today I'm going to make a game of my walk, pretending that my husband is with me. I keep up a steady narrative in my head, explaining the markers and wonders as "we" power up the path over the mountains and through the wash. This way I can experience everything again as though for the first time and keep my memories as palpable as pressed flowers.

Jim proves an excellent companion, content to listen to my endless stream of compressed observances, politely turning his head to note the rusted-out Mustang just past the fork in the wash and the black coal from mining road days mixed in with the dust and gravel. Maddeningly, he instantly sees the paddles of the windmill turning a few hundred yards across the ravine when I point them out. He does not protest taking the long way around and seems impressed with my mastery of the terrain. I explain the marvel Jeanne introduced me to, and we cut across the brush and the drovers' trails to reach the face in the tree. He maintains the proper meditative silence throughout.

This morning there are more lizards slithering around, and out of the corner of my eye I think I've seen a young bobcat, but other than that there are no more animals than usual out and about. I check my watch. Six thirty. If we move really fast we can get back for seven o'clock Eucharist.

After breakfast I take my rosary to the garden and decide to devote each decade to other people and to intentions not my own. I pray for Jim and my sister Leslie that they find faith and peace; for my mother that her mantle of grief over my sister Kim's death lighten; for Kim's ex-fiance, his terminally ill wife, and their daughter; and for my grandfather Louis, whom I have always hated.

It is the first time I've ever prayed for him; for all I know it's the first time anyone has prayed for him since his funeral in 1979. I've imagined him with the fires of hell burning around him and liked it. I wanted him to stay there, as probably most people who'd had any close dealings with him did.

He was a lousy father and left his son, my father, Richard, a lonely closet alcoholic who had difficulty with intimacy. He left his daughter clinically depressed until his death, when all her symptoms magically disappeared and she suddenly became a vivacious world traveler. And he left two of his three wives feeling cheated.

Now I feel that opening my heart to pray for him is an important step in learning to forgive myself. When my rosary is complete, I seek out the silence of my hermitage for yet more reading. I am still soaking in the written word like desert plants soak up dew.

It is odd that I've just prayed for my grandfather, because the book I pick out from my remaining pile outlines the patterns of shame-based relationships. I can easily see the sins of the fathers (and mothers) visited on the children in both my father's and mother's families of origin. I can see them in mine. Part of over-coming this pattern is to see and then forgive. I do see and I want so much to forgive, but for right now I can only pray that I will one day feel real forgiveness, the kind that God feels for me.

God sees all and yet forgives. It is nearly impossible for me to imagine how it would feel to be such an expansive being. To not keep score.

When I finish my reading my watch says it's time for lunch. As usual my book is polite and declines to interfere with my mealtimes. At lunch I see a note with my name on it pinned to the kitchen bulletin board. A fellow retreatant has left me a copy of a Hopi prayer. I read it while silently enjoying my soup at the window near the bird grotto.

After lunch I lie down and fall instantly asleep. I don't remember my dreams but am happy when I wake up. It must be true that naps are grace; Patsy told me so and she is a nun.

My resting is like my books — totally respectful of schedule and prayer. I have just enough time to get to Our Lady of Solitude for meditation. I splash cold water on my sleep-swollen eyes and set out for the humble little pale green chapel with the voluptuous window on the desert.

Before I reach the dying saguaro, I feel the first soft drops of real rain. Every drop scatters a tiny cloud of dust when it hits the earth. The drops are like soft tiny cannon balls bouncing and settling. The birds sing alleluia. I turn my face up to feel the rain. I am laughing but it looks like I am crying because little rivulets are running down the dry wash of my cheeks.

There is no deluge in the offing, no torrent to flood the wash and isolate us at Desert House, turning the grounds into an island. There is no lightning or thunder. This is a quiet rain keeping the solitude with us. The drops feel like holy water. I feel privileged, blessed. My wish has come true! My rain prayers have been granted.

I do an improvised celebratory rain dance on the asphalt patch outside the chapel. Some of the others coming to the Centering Prayer service, during which we silently repeat our mantras, join in. There may be a rule against talking but clearly none against dancing or laughing or joy.

Any remaining sadness washes away. Like the cactus wren and the jackrabbits and the pale green paloverde. I know there are better things to come. Water is growth. Water is life and it is time to drink it in.

We enter the chapel, removing our shoes in preparation for meditation. I am ready with the mantra Father

Kane has given me — "Jesus loves me." With repetition I come to believe it, and when the bells signal it is time for our walk around the chapel, my feet never falter. I can do it with my eyes closed. I can sense the corners to be turned in the chapel and in my life.

After Centering Prayer I stay for Vespers and sing my gratitude for the rain although the rain has already stopped and the sun is shining once again. There will be no occasion to talk about the unusual rain (two weeks early for the rainy season) this evening because today as every Friday all meals are taken in silence. We file out quietly to the kitchen and make up our own plates at the same time the birds outside our screen door are taking time for their own meal.

After washing and clearing, I stop in the dining room to see whether the book collection has any information on desert rain. I find something about phantom rain, or *virga.* It happens when cold air high above the desert unleashes a real downpour from clouds collecting there. Then as the rain falls it enters a layer of much drier hotter air and in a few seconds evaporates. Ours hadn't been phantom rain but it sure disappeared in a hurry. It must have been too strong a rain to be deterred by the hot dry air we've had today and all week.

Or maybe it was a small miracle, a benediction.

I return to Bede to pack. It's good that I am leaving; I'm beginning to feel a little possessive about the place, a bit too attached. And the whole point of this sojourn is to detach. To become comfortable with not having all the answers, to not having real control over anything in this life.

I watch the sun set behind the saguaro crosses on the mountain. Tonight I don't see crucifixion when I look at them, but resurrection.

It's time for prayer and then a last sleep in a strange bed.

Dona Nobis Pacem

> Grant me your peace.
> The peace of the womb.
> The sleep of the just.
> The clarity of the committed.
> The eyes of the guileless.
> The content past desire.

Go in Peace

The routine here is a blessing and I try to maintain it as long as I can before taking off.

I hike, take communion and then breakfast, return my last volume to the library, and then leave thank-you notes on the refectory table for Nick, Sister Patsy, Father Kane, and the rest of the staff. I don't want to forget them and I don't want them to forget me. Besides the notes I've also left a plant, a flowering mutt cactus from a local nursery's strange collection of hybrids.

Like every guest before me, I spend the rest of my time erasing my presence from my room. I dust all the corners of Bede, bathe his floors and scrub his shower and sink, water the plants, rearrange the candles and the pens and papers in the desk, wash and dry the linens, put away the coffeepot and cups. When I finish with Bede, I wish him well.

Then the clay watering dish must be filled for the foxes and cactus wrens, the stoop swept of dust and sand, the white plastic chair placed fetchingly for maximum curb appeal. I want the next guest to feel as at home in the humble little house as I have.

I pack my bags quickly and walk them up to the office.

It's quiet as usual in the common rooms, but as my new friends drift in I discreetly snap their pictures so I can show Jim and the kids who I'm talking about. Later, when the edges of my mental pictures blur, I can look at my photographs and relive much of this experience.

I know despite all our protestations to the contrary that most of us will probably never see each other again. There are the letters we'll never write, the cards we won't send, the calls and visits we'll never make. Maybe none of us have really gotten to know each other at all; maybe some of us already know each other too well. But experience says we won't make the effort to keep the circle unbroken, even if we have shared a sacred time.

There's time before the Arizona Stage is due so I take up the rocker in the little book nook at the back of the common room that faces out toward the Gethsemane Garden and the mountains beyond. It's time to make an assessment of my time in "solitary."

I realize with some surprise that after the first day's panic I never really faced any bouts of discomfort with solitude. Once I let go and let myself sink into the quiet, it felt like falling into a favorite chair. Am I being honest? Well, there *were* those dark episodes right before I sat vigil and just before the rain. But that darkness was a night I needed to enter as fully as I did so I could keep my future days from always being tinged by twilight. Dark and light seem so much easier to deal with than shadow.

I feel lighter than when I came. I seem to have shed the weight of my doppelganger victim. Once I had the chance to be alone and small and afraid again, I realized that I haven't been a victim for a long time and that there was no need to keep carrying that frail creature on my back or even in the back of my mind. I am a tall paloverde with enough shade for all my children and enough arms to hug not only them but also myself. Maybe one day I will be able to wrap my arms around my mother. I am strong and expect to live long enough to grow whatever arms are required. How well the nurse plants and the saguaro mothers have taught me.

Of course, I will continue to nag and chide because the Gambel's quail mother taught me a few things, too. Some things about mothering are both universal and universally resented. Does the quail mother really want to be a pecker and chaser? She knows she must be one and doesn't fight it just as I won't fight it anymore either even if it doesn't fit with my more idealized vision of motherhood.

Nature offered me no lessons on how to be a better spouse. But I hope that in praying for my most significant other, Jim, I will expand my ability to see his universe a little bit better.

I don't feel holy or even holier. But I do feel a stillness at my center. It's a stillness akin to that I felt sitting in the dark in front of Bede. A quiet occasionally interrupted by the low whir of a faraway engine negotiating a bend in my brain.

Now I hear a real engine and go to the front screen window to see that the Arizona Stage has arrived. Trudy emerges from the office and we exchange a small hug.

"I know you'll be back." She says it with such confidence that I'm sure she's right.

The driver comes around from the rear of the van where he's been shuffling luggage, and I see that it's Clint. He doesn't recognize me and I decide not to remind him of our past acquaintance. I don't feel like talking or being examined for signs of a spiritual transformation. There probably aren't any signs he'd accept anyway. My hair's the same length, maybe longer. I haven't decided to become a nun. Clint seems disinclined to play his man of the West role anyway. Today he's very much a man in a hurry, and when he slides open the van door so I can get in I see why; there are already three other passengers inside. They all look sleepy and not much interested in my entrance. One of them politely passes me a bottle of cold water without comment and I nod my thanks.

I don't feel holy or even holier. But I do feel a stillness at my center.

This is as good as a having a van full of retreatants. My silence will extend all the way to Tucson International, maybe all the way home to O'Hare if I'm lucky. As Clint maneuvers the Arizona Stage around and down the long drive we come to the fork, and I turn around in my seat to read my favorite sign: NO HUNTING EXCEPT FOR PEACE.

Peace. I do feel more at peace with my own deficiencies and those of others. But it's easy to be at peace here where there is no chatter to betray your own pettiness and stupidity nor reveal the same qualities in others. It's easy to attribute the silent with more wisdom than they actually possess. The trick will be to be peaceful among the loud and against the shrill, rising voice of my own and others' irritations.

I am lucky. The plane back to Chicago isn't full, and I have a seat all to myself. For now I am all read out so I don't flip through any magazines or open a book. I nap without guilt, a gift from Patsy and Desert House and their belief that naps are a special form of grace. I am Mary in a world of Marthas, the one who gets to sit and do nothing but wait on God's pleasure.

I don't know what's next. I don't think my prayers are dark enough to fit my old book idea anymore. Try as I might, I can't seem to squeeze the hope out of them. I regret that I never studied botany or zoology because I could spend the rest of my life observing plants and animals. Perhaps I am an anthropologist. I will spend the rest of my life keenly observing my children and that should teach me something about what it means to be human and a little of what it means to be me.

Because of Father Kane I seem at last to be able to accept that God loves me. Now what I have to confront is whether I truly love God or even want to. Those who love God are willing to forgo comfort and rewards to serve others, and I have thus far shown no talent for forgoing anything. Serving my children is just another form of serving myself.

I understand now what compelled Jesus to spend forty days in the desert being tempted by the devil. I understand why Mohammed withdrew from the world during the month of Ramadan to the cave of Hera. I understand why Catherine of Siena spent three years in seclusion in her cell in the via Benincasa. Not that I could ever hope to attain their holiness. But like them and like the caterpillar I feel the importance of wrapping one's self in a cocoon of silence before moving on to a better and more beautiful life. A chosen life.

The desert is a perfect place to weave that cocoon. It is so tolerant of mystery and oddity that anything can be thought or sought within it and anything found. Even when it is dry and dusty and seemingly lifeless it always has hidden water running through it. If, like the aloe or the saguaro, one cultivates the deep roots needed to tap into that secret water, a small everyday miracle will occur. You will grow green and feel new water coursing through your veins.

Maybe that's why as happy as I was to see my family, the first thing I did when I saw them waiting in front of the throng at the gate was to let some of that water escape from my eyes.

Epilogue 1

Father Kane
Leaves the Desert

The March 2000 issue of *Exodus,* the Desert House newsletter, carried sad news: Father Kane had died. There were complications after surgery for an aortic aneurysm. I immediately regretted not having visited the retreat campus and him for a fourth time.

His successor, Father Paul Curtin, assured all of us that Father Kane had died in peace surrounded by friends. And he pointed out an odd coincidence. Father Kane kept a print of a painting by Georges Rouault that portrayed the face of Christ in his office. Asked why he chose this portrait he replied, "Because in it I see compassion." Georges Rouault was one of Father Kane's favorite artists. He died in 1958 on February 13 — the same date that Father Kane did.

Father Curtin also noted that John Kane "guided others to God. He encouraged poets and artists and allowed God to cultivate him into the person he became: a masterpiece of nature and grace."

He had certainly encouraged me. My three encounters with Father Kane had bent me in a different direction. At his urging I'd kept a journal of my experiences at Desert House that turned into this book. At his suggestion I'd read books that furthered my spiritual growth. And with his blessing of the first draft of my manuscript, I'd sent it out, confident that any work he approved of would find its way into the world in some way.

He'd already grown weaker by the time of my second visit. It would have been a lot to ask that he read my entire manuscript so I asked him to read only chapter 10, which centered on the spiritual counseling he'd given me during a visit to his office. To my delight he chose to read all of it at once and passed it on to Trudy to read, too.

I asked him whether some of the darker passages bothered him because I didn't want to publish anything that would offend him or hurt Desert House in any way. "How could it offend me?" he asked. "It's truthful." Then he looked at me as though I were a new species of cactus he'd discovered. "It is strange to whom God chooses to grant his gifts." he said and then walked on, alone, in the direction of Sophia, the hermitage trailer where he now lived. (For many years he had lived in Patmos.) He is buried at Liguori, Missouri, alongside his Redemptorist brothers. It at first seemed insensitive that he had been taken from his beloved desert and buried in Midwestern mud. I could almost smell the dank, murky river scent that rose from the Mississippi on humid summer mornings and seeped into one's soul. But maybe Father Kane liked the contrast. And maybe the Redemptorist cemetery was more akin to what his boyhood environment in verdant Portland, Oregon, had been like. He was coming home after a long period in the wilderness no matter how much he'd grown to love that wilderness. And for him the desert was about life, not death. While his body might be in Liguori, his spirit would forever inhabit the place he had founded and shaped.

I was curious to know what was on his headstone so I called the Redemptorists to find out. Father Kane's stone was exactly like all the other stones for the other priests that had died. It bore only his name and the pertinent dates: May 20, 1918, and February 13, 2000.

No inscription of "Jesus Loves Me," his prescriptive mantra for the pain of this world? No words to mark the passage of a man who had guided so many people back to God? Then I realized that the plain-spoken headstone was in perfect consonance with the buildings and the spirit of Desert House.

Epilogue 1

Father Kane was a lantern for the lost, illuminating the darkest nights and darkest thoughts without fear of what he might expose. His mere presence in a room transformed it into sacred space.

I was lucky to have known him.

Epilogue 2

Afterward

It has now been several years since my first visit to Desert House. The two-lane Picture Rocks Road that leads there has more cars now. There are a few more houses and fewer dust devils. And there are more new hermitages on the grounds of the retreat campus itself, several far more comfortable than Bede and boasting fireplaces. Some of the trails I took are now closed to public access.

Father Kane is not there, although his trailers, Patmos and Sophia, are. The new director let me spend an afternoon in Sophia, his most recent residence, so I could call up my memories of him. I sat in Father Kane's rocker on his makeshift porch and felt the peace and joy he exuded.

Desert House remains a sacred place. I could feel its quiet power as soon as I turned in the long drive, and even more strongly as I entered the Chapel of Our Lady of Solitude. And I can still feel its presence in my life, although my life is not as pure and full of silence as I'd hoped it would be.

God has once again sent me busy days and a long to-do list. My life has become like the new Picture Rocks Road — full of comings and goings. My light is on late at night. The children I wanted to be with now want less and less to be with me. They are like the baby saguaros who are becoming taller than their mothers and don't want someone watching over them. Advertising keeps coming in and out of my life and now that it isn't all-consuming, I enjoy it again. Everything seems to have come full circle. I am almost in the same place where I started this journey, but with completely new feelings about where I am standing and new people to stand with me.

It's a pretty nice place to be.

A Retreat Reading List

These books are roughly in the order that I read them. Many I stumbled upon myself, and some I was sent to by Father Kane. You can create your own spiritual stew from the same list of ingredients or improvise upon the basic recipe.

1. *The Artist's Way* by Julia Cameron. As much a psychotherapy session as a catalyst for creativity. I credit it for bringing into the open my desire to return to an earlier self. This book is filled with useful exercises for tapping the past, dreams, and one's own anxieties. It espouses a daily journaling technique called "morning pages." Through this alchemy, seemingly negative life experiences lead to better and more powerful writing and more conscious living. There are also workshops around the country based on the book, with leaders approved by the author.

2. *Six Months Off: How to Plan, Negotiate and Take the Break You Need* by Hope Dlugozima, James Scott, and David

Sharp. Great for daydreaming about a future sabbatical or for practical planning of an imminent one. It suggests various religious, artistic, and spiritual settings designed to jump start new lives. This book led me to the Desert House of Prayer, but the vivid and information-rich descriptions of many other artists' retreats, monasteries, meditation centers, and volunteer opportunities may call you in a different direction. It suggests ways to talk to your boss about a sabbatical and to structure one that is as attractive to your employer as it is to you. A warning: not everyone who takes a long sabbatical wants to go back to life as it was. You may be forced to remap your universe.

3. *Ways of Imperfection* by Simon Tugwell. Explores key themes and writers in Christian spirituality from the early church through the fourteenth century, including commentary from modern Christian writers such as Evelyn Waugh and Dom Hubert von Zeller. This witty British Dominican touches on Macarian homilies, the writings of Augustine, and monastic rules and how they apply to the lay Christian. He offers insights about observing and disciplining our own behavior and thinking always with an eye on God.

4. *The Wisdom of the Desert: Sayings from the Desert Fathers of the Fourth Century* by Thomas Merton. Read this at

daily intervals to set the tone for daily meditation. It is overpowering at one fell swoop. While the Desert Fathers shared a desire to live in the same setting and observe similar spiritual practices, each retained his own strong viewpoint on what sins were deadliest and most tormented him as an individual. For instance, Abba Anthony often wrote and taught about anger.

5. *Cathedral* by Raymond Carver. Good secular short stories providing appropriate counterpoint for heavy religious reading. And then there is the title with its appropriate spiritual undertones. Carver was my teacher at an MFA program at Goddard College in Vermont and a former advertising copywriter so I found his writing especially meaningful.

6. *Peterson First Guide to Birds of North America* by Roger Tory Peterson. Provides grounding for spates of spiritual flight. Reminds one that delight in nature may be the fastest way to form a friendship with God. Too bad it's so heavy (in poundage, not intellectual weight); I'd like to carry it with me at all times. I always seem to need it most when I don't have it.

7. *Collected Works* by Annie Dillard. Prompts closer observance of the natural world. She reinforces how important setting can be to thought. Reading it made

me want to take courses in botany and zoology. This collection contains three of her most popular works: *An American Childhood, This Writing Life,* and *Pilgrim at Tinker Creek.* The idyllic summers she describes in her paean to her childhood might provoke a bout with the demon envy because they were so perfect in their unstructured freedom and unlimited contact with nature. You'll wish you'd had her childhood and want the same one for your children.

8. *Letting Go of Shame* by Patricia Potter-Efron and Ron Potter-Efron. Cleansing. This book discourages the self-flagellation that internal journeys can generate. How can you believe in God's forgiveness if you can't forgive yourself? The authors explore the sources of shame in such illuminating ways that I was willing to read it twice, albeit with some ten years between readings.

9–10. *All Hallow's Eve* and *Descending Figure* by Louise Gluck. Poetry whose terse metaphors inspire a deeper look at nature and self. Gluck was my teacher in the same MFA program through which I met Raymond Carver.

11. *Alive Together: New and Selected Poems* by Lisel Mueller. Pulitzer Prize winner's poetry explores relationships and their meaning. Many of the poems use music as

a stepping-off point. The death of the author's mother triggered her need to understand more about love and dying, which is reflected in some of her most poignant lines, such as this one from "In Passing": "as if what exists, exists / so that it can be lost / and become precious." Mueller was my teacher at Elmhurst College.

12. *Collected Works* by W. H. Auden. For sheer beauty of construction and language. Even in silence there is value in words.

13. *Poems of Gerard Manley Hopkins* by Gerard Manley Hopkins. Poetry that parallels Hopkins's conversion to Catholicism. His love of the natural world and love of God become seamless in these verses. He proves the line between prayer and poetry is very, very thin. "Pied Beauty" is a poem I've committed to memory for its ability to make me profoundly happy to be alive even in fairly dark periods.

14. *The Complete Poems of Emily Dickinson* by Emily Dickinson. Thomas H. Johnson, editor. Tight construction that makes you glad God created poets. I think reading Dickinson encourages you to think more potently.

15. *Praying with Catherine of Siena* by Patricia Mary Vinje. A guide to meditationand the cultivation of a pro-

gressive prayer life that is based on this saint's life philosophy of contemplation in action. Catherine's Opening Prayer is a nearly perfect one for being granted a fulfilling life.

16. *The Hermitage Journals* by John Howard Griffin. Personal diaries he kept while working on his biography of Thomas Merton offer insights into the author, Merton, and our own spiritual journeys. This book is the source of a quote from Cassian that I loved: "We pray best when we no longer know we are praying."

17. *How to Meditate* by Sebastian Temple. Teacher about Tratac (an unusual meditation technique that requires concentrating on a blue light) and comparative meditation methods. However, this is not a must-read.

18. *An Anthology of the Love of God* by Evelyn Underhill. Collected insights by a female Anglican mystic, who is widely considered to be one of the twentieth century's greatest. This volume addresses sanctity, the cultivation of inner grace, determining one's purpose in life, and hearing God's call. Says Underhill: "The cleansing and transforming power of suffering abides not in the degree of pain experienced, but in the degree of acceptance achieved."

19. *A Tree Full of Angels: Seeing the Holy in the Ordinary* by Marina Wiederkehr. Personal spiritual journey, portions of which were written at the Desert House of Prayer. The author makes the Benedictine practice of divine reading accessible for everyone. Beautiful phrases and metaphors abound. For example: "When I want to see clearly I close my eyes."

20. *The Seven Storey Mountain* by Thomas Merton. An unlikely journey to a spiritual vocation, which is even better the second time around. This book speaks to me more than many of his later works because it is here that he is most spiritually unevolved and most conscious of his status as a sinner. I'd forgotten that he'd fathered a "love child" while at Cambridge.

21–23. *Falling Off, The Middle of the World,* and *Little Girls in Church* by Kathleen Norris. The poetic career that preceded and complements *Dakota, A Spiritual Geography, The Cloister Walk,* and *Amazing Grace.*

24. *Interior Castle* by Teresa of Avila. A celebrated work of mystical theology by a Carmelite nun that compares a soul to a castle with many levels of prayer. Perhaps because several centuries later so many have co-opted her images, I found little freshness or illumination in her analogies. The text was difficult to read because it

was so repetitious and convoluted and the metaphors often mixed. I passed the book on to my mother, an avid spiritual reader who has tackled many difficult volumes, without giving my opinion. After reading it she reported that even though she admired St. Teresa as a person, she found the book uninspiring. I agree.

25. *Harlots of the Desert* by Benedicta Ward. Stories of the independent women who became revered spiritual guides in a time when women held little status in the world or in the church. They include Ammah Sarah, Mary Magdalene, St. Mary of Egypt, Pelagia, and Maria, niece of Abraham. They risked social ostracism and condemnation when they set off to live unconventional lives on their own, but their exemplary spiritual growth and lives eventually won over the male hierarchy that had been skeptical of their actions. This book nicely balances out the stories of the "good girls" of early Christianity such as Marcella, Eugenia, Macrina, and Melania.

26. *Muslim Women Mystics* by Margaret Smith. This story of Rabi'a of Basra, a Sufi and mystic of the eighth century who came to prominence at a time when women were accorded equal status with men saints in Islam. She was devoted to a life of prayer and insight. It is interesting to see the parallels in Christian and Muslim

thought regarding the path to knowing God's will and feeling God's love.

27. *God Was in This Place and I Did Not Know: Finding Self, Spirituality and Ultimate Meaning* by Lawrence Kushner. Reflections on the Bible verse (Genesis 28:16) of the title, which is what Jacob exclaimed when he awoke from his vision of angels ascending and descending the ladder to heaven. Kushner explores interpretations of the verse from a third-century Palestinian to an eighteenth-century woman rabbi from Poland because he believes "biblical words shatter and rearrange themselves before our sustained gaze." They always offer new meanings and insights.

28. *Visions and Longings: Medieval Women Mystics* by Monica Furlong. Features the writings and thoughts of eleven women mystics on religious matters and communion with God from a time when such thoughts by women were ignored and discouraged. Heloise, Hildegard of Bingen, Clare of Assisi, Catherine of Siena, Julian of Norwich, and Margery Kemp are some of the better known names.

29. At Father Kane's suggestion I also read smatterings from some volumes which truly deserved complete readings. Reading in smorgasbord fashion results from

having so many books to read and so little time in which to read them. *Hildegard von Bingen's Mystical Visions* by Hildegard von Bingen, *Revelations of the Divine* by Julian of Norwich, and *The Ladder of Divine Ascent* by John Climacus are among those I only skimmed.

Be sure to take a walk in the woods or down the block between books. My mother was right about going outside for fresh air. Otherwise your brain gets so knotted you can't untangle one book's premise from the next.

Saints, Mystics, and Others Whose Names Grace Desert House

Traveling from Sunset to Sunrise Around the Perimeter of the Property

Dom Bede Griffiths. A priest who married Roman Catholic beliefs with the practices of Eastern mysticism because he felt that in the East he discovered "the other half of my soul." He founded a Benedictine monastic ashram in India and believed that the face of Christ was hidden in all the religions of the world.

Jean Vanier. A living Canadian Christian lecturer and leader who founded L'Arche, a community for men and women with developmental disabilities. In a society that values production and competition, he feels the "handicapped" teach us the value of sharing, acceptance, and joy. He believes that "community is not built upon heroic actions but rather upon the love shown in the little things of everyday life."

Dorothy Day. American founder of the Catholic Worker lay movement, which set out to show that the radical gospel commandment of love could be lived in the modern world. She offered food and shelter for those suffering during the Depression and sought social justice for all. She believed that the poor are Jesus, and that what we do to them we do to him.

John Patmos. A first-century visionary and prophet who received the Revelation of the Apocalypse while living in isolation on the Greek isle of Patmos in the Aegean Sea.

Catherine of Siena. A fourteenth-century holy woman. During her self-confinement to a cell of prayer and self-knowledge, she experienced ecstatic union with God. Her spiritual gifts led her to act in the role of peacemaker between warring factions and cities in the church of the mid-fourteenth century at a time when few women could attain such status.

Thomas Merton. A prolific author, Trappist monk, and promoter of a contemplative life that kept itself open to the world. He was a student and practitioner of Eastern mysticism who believed that the gate of heaven can be found everywhere in everyday life if we choose to open it.

Charles de Foucauld. An aristocrat who became a Trappist monk because Christ was poor and a worker. He spent fifteen years in the desert and believed that being alone with God makes us better able to love our neighbors as ourselves because it allows us to see the union between all living beings.

Clement Hofbauer. A Redemptorist of the late eighteenth century and founder of an orphanage in Warsaw. When he went to local pubs to raise money for the orphans, the patrons spat beer upon him. He said, "That was for me; what do you have for my boys?" His Christ-like response so moved these men that they then contributed generously. Also known as the Apostle and Patron of Vienna.

Juan de la Cruz. One of the Catholic Church's greatest mystics. He lived in sixteenth-century Spain during the Inquisition. He was beaten and abused for his beliefs by religious conservatives and envious rivals. His greatest work is *Dark Night of the Soul,* an exploration of the stripping away of ego and self-delusion to forge a closer relationship with God.

Hildegard of Bingen. A Benedictine abbess and visionary of twelfth-century Germany blessed with many gifts. She was an artist, a poet, a musician, a pharmacist, a theologian, a prophet, a doctor, and a preacher. She saw the universe and its inhabitants as rays of God's splendor and music as representative of the intended harmony that Satan disturbed.

Paul the Hermit. A fourth-century Egyptian. He is credited with being the first desert monk. It is said that during his time in the wilderness he was fed bread by the ravens who lived there.

Gerard Majella. An eighteenth-century Italian Redemptorist called "The Father of the Poor," who possessed great powers of discernment and insight. He suffered serious slander that resulted in his being stripped of his religious standing but never spoke against his accuser, who recanted years later.

Maria Celeste Crostarosa. Founder of the Redemptoristine Order in seventeenth-century Italy. She led a simple life of prayer and obedience to conscience that was rewarded by many profound mystical experiences.

Joseph. The earthly father of Christ. He led his small family into exile in Egypt to escape the wrath of Herod. He trusted God's message in his dreams, believed in Mary's chosen status, and never let his ego interfere with his son's special relationship with his Father in heaven.

Teresa of Avila. A mystic of sixteenth-century Spain and charismatic leader who attracted many followers. Despite her mystical experiences she was able to speak to others in commonsense terms about prayer. "Prayer is nothing but friendly and frequent solitary converse with Him who we know loves us." She founded the Discalced (shoeless) Carmelites and lived a life of poverty despite being born into wealth.

Magdalen. A first-century follower of Christ called "The Apostle to the Apostles" because she witnessed Christ's resurrection and was sent to tell them the good news. She is the woman "from whom seven demons had gone out" and is known as the epitome of the penitent sinner. Popular lore unfairly branded her as a prostitute.

Ann. Jesus's maternal grandmother. She received and believed a message from an angel promising a daughter would be born to her who would be filled with the Holy Spirit and that she should name her Mary, this despite her age and supposed barrenness.

Francis of Assisi. An Italian saint who lived in the early thirteenth century. He heeded the voice of God, which urged him to "repair my church." He embraced poverty and preached nonviolence in the age of the Crusades. He received the mark of the stigmata while engaged in intense prayer and always tended the needs of the least of God's little ones. He wrote "The Canticle of Creation."

Julian of Norwich. A fourteenth-century mystic who lived a solitary life in a little cell attached to a church. Her visions are marked by their containment of opposites: she saw the crown of thorns as a sign of the sweetness of God's love, the cross as a sign of Christ's friendliness, and his bleeding head as evidence of the depths of God's love. Thus she was able to look into the heart of darkness unafraid and see only the power and love that leads to our redemption.

Morning Star. One of the titles of Our Lady, found in the Litany of the Blessed Virgin Mary, along with "Mystical Rose," "Cause of Our Joy," and "Tower of David."

Adeodata. Latin for "gift of God." It is also the name of St. Augustine's son (Adeodatus), who was born before his conversion and died when very young.

Sophia. Greek for "The Wisdom of God's Word." The name of Father John Kane's hermitage trailer home.

Acknowledgments

This book has had a long, strange journey to publication. There are many people to thank for its continued existence.

Primarily, my editor, Roy M. Carlisle, of Crossroad Carlisle Books, who wouldn't let it die and wouldn't let it be published by anyone but him. Also, Jan-Erik Guerth, my former agent and initial editor, who offered invaluable insight and support. And Father John Kane, who persuaded me that an uncredentialed layperson should write a book about the silent retreat experience.

Sister Joy, Sister Genny, and Father Paul Curtin of Desert House kept me accurate, gave me access, and contended with my faxes. Thank you also to my early readers: author James Patterson, James Licata, Betsey Dalbeck, Carol Gold-Lande, Sandy Wade, Mark Silveira, Lisa Von Drehle, Renee Bernhard, and Father John Kane.

Acknowledgments

I am in awe of the generosity of many in the publishing world: Jennifer Westwood, for including my essay about this experience in her book *On Pilgrimage: Sacred Journeys around the World* (Hidden Spring, 2003); Tamara Traeder; Paulette Millichap; Frank Cunningham; Carol Brown; and Mark Greenberg.

And I am most grateful for the support of my publisher, Gwendolin Herder, and the fast-moving staff at Crossroad.

My mother is responsible for making me a Reader. My husband, James Licata, encouraged me to keep writing even when it seemed futile. I also thank my children, Fabiana, Viveca, and Julian, for pushing me out of the advertising world and into another one.

All that's left to say is this: glory be to God for dry, odd things.

About the Author

Rita Winters is a wife, mother, writer, and advertising executive who stepped off the multinational advertising agency fast track for several years to better connect with her family, her God, and herself. To make this transition she spent several weeks in silence in the Sonoran Desert in Arizona.

Although she was baptized Roman Catholic, Rita is a convert to the Episcopal Church. Ms. Winter's writing and experience is rooted in formal Christianity but is enriched by the writings of other religions and faiths.

She lives in Chicago with her husband and children and juggles even more than she did before, but is grateful for the brief chance she had to live in silence and the effect it has had on her striving to be in the world but not of it.

Ms. Winters holds a BA in English from Elmhurst College in Illinois and has also taken classes in the MFA Program in Writing at Goddard College in Vermont. Rita was a contributor to Jennifer Westwood's *On Pilgrimage*. Ms. Winters is currently working on a book of prayers.

OF RELATED INTEREST

Paula D'Arcy
THE GIFT OF THE RED BIRD
A Spiritual Encounter

When Paula D'Arcy lost her husband and baby in a car crash, she began an inner search for a faith that was stronger than fear. In *Gift of the Red Bird* she shares her remarkable spiritual adventure: Paula literally journeyed alone into the wilderness for three days, allowing the Creator to speak through that creation. As she surrendered to the power of God alone, a red bird appeared and, without words, began to teach...

"To say that *The Gift of the Red Bird* moved me deeply seems inadequate. I wept for its beauty, pain, and joy. It is a powerful testimony to how the Divine woos the soul into a sacred embrace. Paula D'Arcy's vulnerability and courage in narrating her true story of this Divine encounter are remarkable."   — Joyce Rupp

"It is all a matter of seeing but we need seers to show us how. Paula D'Arcy shatters our poor sight and shows us light."
— Richard Rohr

0-8245-1956-6, $14.95 paperback

crossroad

OF RELATED INTEREST

Paula D'Arcy
A NEW SET OF EYES
Encountering the Hidden God

Through a series of meditations and parables, D'Arcy helps readers awaken the mind to the presence of God, free the soul from its cherished idols, and infuse the emotions with joy. By the popular author of *Gift of the Red Bird* and *Song for Sarah*.

0-8245-1930-2, $16.95 hardcover

Paula D'Arcy
SEEKING WITH ALL MY HEART
Encountering God's Presence Today

A verse in Jeremiah promises that the seemingly elusive God will be found when "you search for me with all your heart." This collection of reflections and meditations is such a search — a search that has taken D'Arcy through both New and Old Testaments, honored writings, as well as the reaches of her own experience. D'Arcy shows contemporary spiritual seekers that when we meditate on these verses, our sense of time disappears and there is only now. They speak, if you're willing to know and to see differently.

0-8245-2109-9, $19.95 hardcover

crossroad